Survival Analysis

POCKET GUIDES TO
SOCIAL WORK RESEARCH METHODS

Series Editor
Tony Tripodi, DSW
Professor Emeritus, Ohio State University

Determining Sample Size:
Balancing Power, Precision, and Practicality
Patrick Dattalo

Preparing Research Articles
Bruce A. Thyer

Systematic Reviews and
Meta-Analysis
Julia H. Littell, Jacqueline Corcoran,
and Vijayan Pillai

Historical Research
Elizabeth Ann Danto

Confirmatory Factor Analysis
Donna Harrington

Randomized Controlled Trials:
Design and Implementation for
Community-Based Psychosocial
Interventions
Phyllis Solomon, Mary M.
Cavanaugh, and Jeffrey Draine

Needs Assessment
David Royse,
Michele Staton-Tindall,
Karen Badger,
and J. Matthew Webster

Multiple Regression with Discrete
Dependent Variables
John G. Orme and Terri
Combs-Orme

Developing Cross-Cultural
Measurement
Thanh V. Tran

Intervention Research:
Developing Social Programs
Mark W. Fraser, Jack M. Richman,
Maeda J. Galinsky,
and Steven H. Day

Developing and Validating Rapid
Assessment Instruments
Neil Abell, David W. Springer, and
Akihito Kamata

Clinical Data-Mining:
Integrating Practice and Research
Irwin Epstein

Strategies to Approximate Random
Sampling and Assignment
Patrick Dattalo

Analyzing Single System Design Data
William R. Nugent

The Dissertation:
From Beginning to End
Peter Lyons and Howard J. Doueck

Survival Analysis
Shenyang Guo

SHENYANG GUO

Survival Analysis

OXFORD
UNIVERSITY PRESS

2010

OXFORD

UNIVERSITY PRESS

Oxford University Press, Inc., publishes works that further
Oxford University's objective of excellence
in research, scholarship, and education.

Oxford New York
Auckland   Cape Town   Dar es Salaam   Hong Kong   Karachi
Kuala Lumpur   Madrid   Melbourne   Mexico City   Nairobi
New Delhi   Shanghai   Taipei   Toronto

With offices in
Argentina   Austria   Brazil   Chile   Czech Republic   France   Greece
Guatemala   Hungary   Italy   Japan   Poland   Portugal   Singapore
South Korea   Switzerland   Thailand   Turkey   Ukraine   Vietnam

Copyright © 2010 by Oxford University Press, Inc.

Published by Oxford University Press, Inc.
198 Madison Avenue, New York, New York 10016

www.oup.com

Library of Congress Cataloging-in-Publication Data

Guo, Shenyang.
Survival analysis / Shenyang Guo.
p.   cm. — (Pocket guides to social work research methods)
Includes bibliographical references and index.
ISBN 978-0-19-533751-8
1. Event history analysis.   2. Social sciences—Statistical methods.
I. Title.
H61.G868 2010
300.72'7—dc22
2009022503

1   3   5   7   9   8   6   4   2

Printed in the United States of America
on acid-free paper

Acknowledgments

T his book is primarily a product of my experiences with a five-year study investigating the impact of welfare reform on child welfare (Co-Principal Investigator Kathleen Wells and Co-Principal Investigator Shenyang Guo) sponsored by the Annie E. Casey Foundation, the Gund Foundation, and the Cleveland Foundation; and my six years of teaching a course on longitudinal methods at the University of North Carolina at Chapel Hill. I specially thank Kathleen Wells for her expertise in theories, child welfare policies, and research methodology, whose innovative ideas and rigorous research spirit make the illustrating examples for this book possible. I thank Dean Jack Richman, the Associate Dean Mark Fraser, and the former Chair of the Doctoral Program Richard Barth at the School of Social Work at UNC for their support of my course on longitudinal methods. I received invaluable comments, suggestions, and direct help from Danyu Lin and Paul Allison when conducting and teaching survival analysis. I thank two anonymous reviewers for their invaluable suggestions and comments on an earlier version of this book. Finally, I thank my wife, Shenyan Li, and children, Han and Hanzhe, for their support, understanding, and patience.

Contents

Survival Analysis

1

Introduction

S urvival analysis is a collection of statistical methods used to address questions that have to do with whether and when an event of interest takes place. Precisely, it is "the analysis of data that correspond to the time from a well-defined *time origin* until the occurrence of some particular event or *end-point*" (Collett, 1994, p. 1). Time-to-event data are ubiquitous in social work research. For instance, child welfare researchers and practitioners are concerned about the length of time children stay in foster homes because federal law (i.e., the Adoption and Safe Families Act, Public Law 105-89) requires reasonable efforts to find homes for foster children within 12 months that are safe, permanent, and provide adequate nutrition. In studying welfare reform, researchers are concerned about factors affecting the length of time recipients use Temporary Assistance for Needy Families (TANF) because the Personal Responsibility and Work Opportunity Reconciliation Act (Public Law 104–193) mandates a lifetime limit of 60 months for any recipient using TANF. In evaluating mental health treatment interventions, researchers and practitioners closely monitor the timing of relapse of targeted problems because reducing the incidences and determining the timing of relapse are key measures of the interventions' effectiveness.

In all these instances, the timing of event occurrence is a key interest in research. Because the time-to-event data involve *censoring*, a crucial difference of this type of data from cross-sectional data, conventional statistical approaches cannot be readily employed. Definition and details of censoring will be provided in Chapter 2. At the present time, let's simply consider censoring as a problem of incomplete data, that is, researchers cannot observe the entire histories of the targeted event for all study subjects and are unable to determine exactly the timing of event occurrence for a portion of study subjects. At any point by which researchers conclude their data collection, they always have a group of subjects whose exact times of having a defined event are unknown. The fact that the event has not yet occurred for certain subjects at the time when data collection is completed does not exclude the possibility that such an event will occur to them in the future. What the researchers observe from the data set is that the time to event for the censored subjects is greater than a certain number of time units (say months); and among them, some will experience the event in the future, and some will never experience it. In this setting, time to event is known to be censored at a specific value.

In quantitative research, data analysts typically conduct univariate, bivariate, and multivariate analyses to test research hypotheses. After data collection, they typically begin with a univariate analysis by using statistics such as mean, median, or standard deviation to discern central tendency or dispersion of the study variables; they then conduct bivariate analysis such as an independent-sample t test, chi-square test, correlation analysis, or analysis of variance (ANOVA) to examine the association between an outcome variable and an explanatory variable; and finally, they test research hypotheses regarding the net impact of an explanatory variable on the outcome variable by conducting a multivariate analysis such as an ordinary least squares (OLS) regression—that is, by controlling for all other explanatory variables they ask how much change they observe in the outcome by changing one unit in the explanatory variable (Guo, 2008).

Because of censoring, all approaches described above are invalid in analysis of time-to-event data. Instead, researchers should use a special type of statistical model, known as survival analysis, to analyze such data. Specifically, instead of using mean, median, and standard deviation, researchers should use quantiles (such as the 50 percentile or 75 percentile) of survivor function estimated by a Kaplan-Meier (or a life-table method) to conduct univariate analysis; use the estimated variance (equivalently the estimated standard error) of the quantile, such as that estimated by Greenwood's estimator, to perform a special type of bivariate tests (i.e., the log-rank and Wilcoxon tests) to discern whether group differences observed on survivor functions are statistically significant; and use a special type of regression model such as a discrete-time model, a Cox proportional hazards model, or a parametric regression model to conduct multivariate analysis.

Describing this type of statistical analysis (i.e., modified models designed to handle censoring induced by the time-to-event data) is the central theme of this book. The term *survival analysis* comes from biomedical researchers because the methods originate from biomedical interests in studying mortality, or patients' survival times between the time of diagnosis of certain disease and death. Indeed, the first survival analysis was conducted approximately 350 years ago, when John Graunt (1620–1674, son of a London draper) derived the very first life table and published his famous paper "Natural and Political Observations Made Upon the Bills of Mortality" in 1662. In this landmark work that might today be considered biostatistical research, Graunt investigated the risk inherent in the processes of birth, marriage, and death (i.e., the demographic dynamics) and employed weekly reports on the numbers and causes of death in suburban London to compare one disease with another and one year with another by calculating mortality statistics (Everitt, 2005a).

Survival analysis has different names in different disciplines; sociologists call it event history analysis (Tuma & Hannan, 1984; Yamaguchi, 1991), economists call it duration analysis or transition analysis (Greene, 2003; Heckman & Singer, 1985), and engineering researchers call it lifetime or failure-time analysis (Lawless, 1982). Among them, survival analysis is most popularly used, and for this reason this book adopts the term.

Ever since the publication of the seminal paper of Cox (1972) that signified a milestone of modern survival analysis, an enormous number of textbooks and journal articles have discussed the statistical theories and application issues of survival analysis. This book aims to accomplish two objectives in describing survival analysis: *(a)* to make the statistical principles and application strategies more accessible to general researchers, and *(b)* to illustrate the applications of survival analysis to social work research. Hence, the book was designed to fit strictly the definition of the Pocket Guides to Social Work Research Methods. For this reason, I will avoid derivations of statistical theorems, though I will offer important references for this kind of information. It is recommended that readers who need to find methodological details consult these texts.

WHY AND WHEN SURVIVAL ANALYSIS IS NEEDED

The dependent variable of any survival analysis typically contains two pieces of information, which makes it categorically different from the dependent variables used in conventional statistical analysis. The first piece of such data is a continuous variable recording the actual time (days, months, quarters, or years) the study subjects experience a change process, and the second piece is a dichotomous variable indicating a change of state (i.e., changing from state 1, "the absence of a defined event," to state 2, "the presence of such an event"). Although in practice, the categorical piece of the dependent variable may have various names (i.e., it's sometimes called *event code*, and sometimes called *censoring code*), the dependent variables of all survival models share this feature of dual-piece information, and because of this, the analysis is also called a *continuous-duration-and-discrete-state* model.

The first task in any statistical analysis is to choose an appropriate statistical method that fits the type of research questions asked and the nature of data researchers have at hand. As explained earlier, because of censoring, conventional statistical models are invalid in analysis of time-to-event data, and researchers must employ survival analysis in these cases. To answer the question of when and why an analysis needs to apply a survival model, I created a hypothetical sample of seven TANF recipients whose lengths of time of using the TANF program during a 12-month study period were accurately recorded. Of these seven recipients, we know exact time of using TANF only for subjects A, C, and E. For subject F, by the time the 12-month study window ends, we have not observed event occurrence (i.e., exiting from the TANF roll); the only information available to us is that the subject's length of using TANF is greater than 12 months. For subjects B and D, because they moved to other states, we don't know whether they continued to use TANF in those states. Subject G could not remember exactly when she had started to use TANF at the time of data

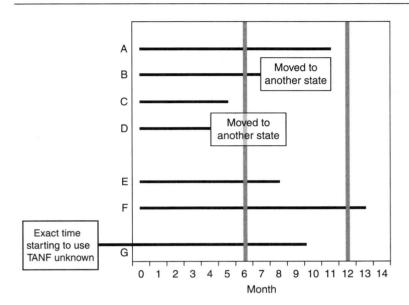

Figure 1.1 Length of time using TANF for hypothetical sample of seven recipients.

collection; however, we knew that subject G had one child 14 months old, so her length of time using TANF could not be greater than 14 months because having a dependent child is a basic requirement for eligibility to receive TANF. Of these seven recipients, event times for subjects B, D, F, and G are censored. If our study window is shortened to 6 months (i.e., if we are more interested in whether subjects exited from TANF within 6 months than 12 months), then the event time for subject E is also censored.

With these kinds of data and within the conventional statistical procedures, researchers have the following two choices of analytical models, and each has noteworthy limitations:

1. Researchers run a logistic regression model to seek predictors of the proportion of subjects exiting the program within a fixed time period (i.e., either a 6-month period or a 12-month period). Using logistic regression, researchers know that 2 of the 7 recipients (28.6%) used TANF fewer than 6 months, or that 5 of the 7 recipients (71.4%) used TANF fewer than 12 months, and whether

one recipient whose length of time is shorter than 12 months is unknown. Using this model, researchers cannot distinguish long-time users such as subject A (or F) from short-time users such as subject C. In conducting a longitudinal inquiry, the most important research question is not "how many" or "what is the proportion exiting TANF" but "when" and "how long" it took them to exit. A logistic regression cannot answer this type of timing question.

2. Researchers run an OLS regression to seek length of stay on TANF. In such a model, subjects B, D, and F are problematic if one uses 12 months as a study window; and all subjects except C become problematic if one uses 6 months as a window. Event times for these subjects are censored, and the multiple regression analysis would treat these subjects' event times as *completely observed* and noncensored.

Researchers using survival analysis may have different substantive interests in different study contexts. However, they all share a common interest: describing *whether* events occur and *when* events occur. Because of this characteristic, Singer and Willett (2003) recommend conducting "the whether and when test" to determine whether a research question calls for the use of survival analysis. If a research question includes either word—whether or when—the research probably needs to use survival analysis. Using this test, Singer and Willett illustrate three different types of research questions (i.e., a study examining time to relapse among recently treated alcoholics, a study investigating how long special educators stay in teaching and factors associated with teachers' decision to stay or leave, and a study determining the age at which young Americans start to have suicide ideation) that all pass the "whether and when test," and they show the importance of using survival analysis rather than conventional models in these studies.

SIGNIFICANCE OF CONDUCTING SURVIVAL ANALYSIS

The foremost importance of conducting survival analysis is the need to understand change and the unique advantage of longitudinal inquiry over cross-sectional inquiry. The distinguishing feature of a longitudinal inquiry is that the response variable of interest and a set of explanatory variables (factors and/or covariates) in such studies are measured repeatedly over time. The main objective of a longitudinal inquiry is to characterize change in the response variable over time and to determine the covariates most associated with any change (Everitt, 2005b). Precisely, when social and health researchers use the term *longitudinal inquiry*, they refer to three characteristics distinguishing it from cross-sectional inquiry. First, it signifies a shift from the point-in-time perspective to a cohort or time-series perspective. As such, selection bias due to a narrowed focus on a single time segment is overcome. Second, it aims to explain the effect of time on a particular outcome for individuals under study by explicitly disentangling three types of effects: age, period, and cohort (Fienberg & Mason, 1979). In this setting, *age* reflects physiological change during a life process; *period* denotes the date of the outcome, and if the outcome varies with period whether the variation is likely due to some underlying factor that affects the outcome and varies in the same way for the entire population under study; and *cohort* refers to generational effects caused by factors that only affect particular groups when their outcome level changes with time (Holford, 2005). And finally, longitudinal inquiry employs analytical methods specifically designed to respond to challenges imposed by the longitudinal data, such as survival models that address the censoring problem, growth curve analysis that corrects for clustering effect, and autoregressive time series models that correct for temporal autocorrelations. Among the three features (i.e., addressing the censoring problem, correcting the clustering effect, and correcting the temporal autocorrelations), development and application of longitudinal models plays a critical role.

The roots of scientific interest in studying change date back 2,500 years to the ancient Greek philosopher Heraclitus, who claimed, "You could not step twice into the same river, for other waters are ever flowing onto you" (Wikipedia, 2008). Robust analytic methods (particularly those for studying change in social behavioral phenomena), however, were not available until very recently. Survival analysis is one of such methods developed to facilitate analysis of longitudinal data, particularly data produced by cohort designs, and it has proven to be useful for addressing many research questions concerning timing-of-event occurrence.

To provide a sense of the importance and utility of survival analysis in social work research, I show below examples drawn from the literature across a variety of social work areas. Survival analysis is suitable to all these studies, and indeed, shows unique advantages over cross-sectional analysis. The research questions of these studies all center on timing-of-event occurrence; as a consequence, the implications drawn by these studies are profound to policy making, knowledge building, and practices that are evidence-based.

Example 1: Assessing the speed of foster children's reunification with family using a cohort approach that overcomes the selection bias embedded in the point-in-time approach. Up to the late 1980s, the dominant approach in evaluating foster care outcomes in child welfare research was cross-sectional or point-in-time. Goerge (1990) criticized the point-in-time approach, particularly the selection bias embedded in the Mars and Engler study evaluating number of children exiting from substitute care, and employed survival analysis to evaluate factors affecting the children's reunification with family. The most significant contribution Goerge's study makes is to employ administrative data to follow a group of children who entered foster care at approximately the same time (i.e., using a cohort approach), and to examine factors affecting the "speed" with which they achieved family reunification. As such, the study enables researchers to answer the key question puzzling most policy makers and child welfare practitioners: why did certain groups of foster children reunify with their families at earlier time points (i.e., stayed in foster care for a shorter period of time, or have a faster speed of making the change from staying in foster care to achieving family reunification) than other groups? Because data collected with a cohort approach inevitably involve censoring, Goerge employed a parametric approach of survival analysis (i.e., a method described in Chapter 5 of this book). Results of such analysis have proved to be fruitful.

Example 2: Assessing foster care outcomes using the Cox proportional hazards model. Ever since Goerge's work, child welfare researchers have employed survival analysis to address a variety of questions directly concerning the safety, well-being, and permanency issues of foster children and have produced numerous studies using the Cox proportional hazards model (i.e., a method described in Chapter 4 of this book). Indeed, studying the timing at which various foster care outcomes occur is one of the most vibrant areas in social work research using survival analysis. Guo and Wells (2003) identified, by the time they concluded their study, 10 studies that used the Cox proportional hazards model to study the length of stay in foster care prior to exit or length of stay at home prior to entry or reentry into foster care. Table 1.1 displays the

Table 1.1 Previous Studies of Foster Care Outcomes That Employed Cox Proportional-Hazards Model

References	Research Objective	Data Source	Sample	Dependent Variable	Significant Independent Variables

• Benedict, White, & Stallings, 1987
 	
• Benedict & White, 1991
	To examine the impact of selected child, family, and agency service factors in explaining children's length of stay in foster care	Social service records from Maryland State Social Services Department	A random sample of 689 children in three predominantly urban/suburban jurisdictions in Maryland between 1/1/1980 and 12/31/1983. The random sample was stratified for age at entry, race, and jurisdiction	Length of stay in foster care for the first time from the day of placement until the day of reunification, adoption, or placement with guardianship using June 1986 as a censoring point (i.e., an observation window of 2.5 to 6 years)	*Finding from the 1987 publication:*
					• African American children did not differ significantly in length of stay from white children
					
					Findings from the 1991 publication:
					• Child factors:
					  Developmental delay
					  Placed with relative
					  Poor school grades
					• Family factors:
					  Previous use of child protective services
					  Uncooperative
					  Wants child back
					• Services needed to implement plan:
					  Parenting education
					  Regular visiting
					  Guardianship

continued

Table 1.1 (Continued)

References	Research Objective	Data Source	Sample	Dependent Variable	Significant Independent Variables
McMurtry & Lie, 1992	To understand how children's characteristics affect their placement outcomes and how long it takes to achieve the outcomes	Review of written case records drawn from the central office of the Arizona Foster Care Review Board	A stratified random sample (stratified by calendar year of entry) of 775 children who entered foster care in Maricopa County, Arizona, between 1/1/1979 and 12/31/1984 and stayed in foster care for at least 6 months	Length of stay in foster care analyzed by four types of exit: return home, adoption, other success, and failure. The censoring point in the study was 12/31/1986 (i.e. an observation window of 2 to 8 years)	*Exit "Return home":* • Ethnicity "Black" • Presence of disability • Child reason for initial placement *Exit "Adoption":* • Age at time of first placement • Presence of disability • Number of siblings in foster care • Family pays part of foster care costs • Parental visitation during first 2 years in care *Exit "Other Success":* • Age at time of first placement • Child reason for initial placement • Parental visitation during first two years in care

• Fraser, Pecora, Popuang, & Haapala, 1992 • Fraser, Jenson, Kifer, & Popuang, 1994	To identify risk factors associated with service failure for children whose families participated in the HOMEBUILDERS model of Intensive Family Preservation Services	Service data collected from a prospective study of child welfare clients	A sample of 409 children coming from 312 families that participated in the HOMEBUILDERS program located in four sites in the state of Washington	Service failure event that was defined as time staying at home, recorded in elapsed days, to any placement in substitute care. The study used a 1-year follow-up period	Exit *"Failure"*: • Ethnicity "Black" • Age at time of first placement • Presence of disability • Child in home at intake • Parental desire to prevent placement low • Child's physical needs high • Child is between ages 13 & 17 • Ethnic minority • Mean goal achievement • Parental mental health poor • Child has at least one prior placement
Courtney, 1994	To explore the child, family, and foster care system variables that are associated with the timing of reunification	Administrative data from California's Foster Care Information System	A random sample of 8,748 children from all children who entered foster care in California between January 1988 and May 1991	Duration of the first foster care episode within a 3-year period with the exit event defined as reunification	*For children initially placed with non-kin:* • Home from which the child was removed: other relative • Health: health problems • Poverty: AFDC eligible

continued

Table 1.1 (Continued)

References	Research Objective	Data Source	Sample	Dependent Variable	Significant Independent Variables
					• Removal reason: sexual abuse • Age at entry: 4–6, 7–12 • Ethnicity: African Americans • Interactions: ethnicity by age; ethnicity by region; remove reason by age *For children initially placed with kin:* • Preplacement services: no services • Home from which the child was removed: both parents • Poverty: AFDC eligible • Region: rural • Ethnicity: Latino; other ethnicity • Interactions: ethnicity by age; ethnicity by region

Study	Purpose	Data source	Sample	Outcome	Factors

Courtney, 1995	To explore the effects of selected child, family, and foster care system factors on reentry	Administrative data from California's Foster Care Information System	A criterion sample of 6,831 children who were discharged from a first episode in foster care in California between 1/1/1988 and 6/30/1988. Criteria used to select cases: children had been returned to biological parents or other kin; age 16 years or younger at the time of discharge	The timing of reentry into foster care within 3 years	• Age at exit from care: 7–12 years
					• Ethnicity: African American
					• Health problems
					• Poverty: AFDC eligible
					• Last placement before discharge: Kin/guardian
					• Placement stability: number of placements
					• Time in care before discharge:
					  ○ 4–6 months
					  ○ 7–12 months
					  ○ 13–24 months
					  ○ Over 24 months

Courtney & Wong, 1996	To examine the relationships between child, family, and service factors and the timing of three exits (i.e., discharge to family or guardian, adoption, and running away) from substitute care	Administrative data generated by child welfare authorities in California	A criterion sample of 8,625 children from the cohort of children who entered a first episode in the foster care system in California between 1/1/80 and 6/30/80. Criteria for sample selection: one child	Duration in foster care within a window of 4.5 to 5 years. Three types of exits were analyzed: discharge to family or guardian, adoption, and running away	*Discharge to family or guardians:* • Age at entry • Ethnicity: African American • Health problems • Poverty: AFDC eligible • Preplacement services • Removal reason: sexual abuse

continued

Table 1.1 (Continued)

References	Research Objective	Data Source	Sample	Dependent Variable	Significant Independent Variables
			from each sibling group, age 16 or younger at entry, and children with valid data		• Removal reason: physical abuse • Removal reason: other reasons • Region: rural • Type of placement: group home • Type of placement: guardian • Type of placement: kinship home *Adoption:* • Age at entry • Ethnicity: Latino • Ethnicity: African American • Health problems • Poverty: AFDC eligible • Preplacement services • Preplacement services • Removal reason: physical abuse

Authors	Purpose	Data source	Sample	Variables
Fraser, Walton, Lewis, Pecora, & Walton, 1996	To describe findings from an evaluation of a program developed to reunify foster	Public agency's child-in-custody placement history data plus reports from the	A random sample of 57 children whose families received an experimental family reunification service	The timing of reunification and returning to foster care within 455 consecutive days • Removal reason: other reasons • Region: rural • Region: Los Angeles • Type of placement: group home • Type of placement: guardian • Type of placement: kinship home *Running away:* • Age at entry • Gender: female • Removal reason: other reasons • Type of placement: group home • Type of placement: kinship home *Reunification during the 90-day service period in the FRS treatment group:* • Child age

continued

Table 1.1 (Continued)

References	Research Objective	Data Source	Sample	Dependent Variable	Significant Independent Variables
children with their biological parents		caregivers and caseworkers	and 53 children whose families received "routine services" from four child welfare districts across the state of Utah. Study families were randomly assigned to either the experimental or the control condition. The sampling frame consisted of 41.1% of all children in foster care in those districts		• Percentage of time spent teaching parenting and family problem-solving skills • Percent of time spent in making referrals *Returning to foster care after initial reunification in the FRS treatment group:* • Child initial placement related to ungovernability • Primary caretaker is employed • Primary caretaker age • Number of children previously placed out in the family • Number of prior placements • Average goal achievement during FRS

					• Percent of time spent in making referrals • Percent of time spent teaching parenting and family problem-solving skills
Wells & Guo, 1999	To examine questions pertaining to the child, family, and placement use characteristics associated with timing of reunification, and for those who are reunified, reentry into foster care	Administrative data available from the county public agency's computerized management information system	A criterion sample of 2,616 children from all children who entered into foster care in Cuyahoga County, Ohio in 1992 and in 1993. Three criteria were used to select cases: placement status, date of placement, and age at placement	The timing of reunification within 24 months for the reunification study, and the timing of reentry within 12 months for the reentry study	*Reunification:* • Cohort 1992 • Ethnicity: African American • Presence of health problems • Home – child removed: both parents • Home – child removed: other • Placement reason: neglect • Placement reason: dependency • First placement type: hospital • Interaction: age by African American

continued

Table 1.1 (Continued)

References	Research Objective	Data Source	Sample	Dependent Variable	Significant Independent Variables
					Reentry: • Ethnicity: African American • First placement reason: physical abuse • Number of moves in the first placement • Last placement type: foster home • Last placement type: group home
Glisson, Bailey, & Post, 2000	To identify child, family, and service characteristics that predict the time children spend in state custody in several regions of Tennessee	Service records and additional data collected by the research team weekly on-site over a 3-year period	A random sample of 700 children from those children who entered state custody over a 1-year period in five children's service regions in middle and east Tennessee	Hazard rate (duration) of reunification within a 3-year period	*Main variables:* • Child race African American • Child disabilities • Child sexually abused • Child Behavioral Checklist externalizing score • Family structure precustody: Relative-other • Having siblings in custody • Reason for custody: unruly/delinquent • County: urban

Interactions:
- Reason for custody dependent/neglect–other by age
- Reason for custody unruly-delinquent by age
- Reason for custody unruly-delinquent by gender
- TRF externalizing portion score by age
- CBCL internalizing portion score by parental alcohol and drug abuse

- Gender: Male
- Race: African American
- Race: Hispanic

Kemp & Bodonyi, 2000	To examine length of stay and permanency outcome (legalized adoption or guardianship) of legally free children who were first placed into out-of-home care as infants, focusing specifically on gender and racial and ethnic background as predictors of permanency outcomes	The Washington State Department of Children and Family Services (DCFS) management information system, case record reviews, and individual interviews with DCFS caseworkers and supervisors	A sample of 458 legally free children who were infants (< 1 year old) on the date they were placed in care. The sample was drawn from a larger sample (n = 1,417) that included all children identifiable as legally free in Washington State on June 15, 1995	Length of stay in foster care before achieving permanency (i.e., legalized adoption or guardianship) within a one-year study window

features of each of the studies, listed by year of publication, along with a common set of parameters: the research objective, the source of data, the features of the sample, the dependent variable (i.e., length of time and event of interest), and the independent variables having a statistically significant relation to the dependent variable. Notice that significant predictors of timing of desirable foster care outcomes (such as timing of reunification), or of timing of undesirable foster care outcomes (such as timing of entry or reentry into foster care) are important information about an accountable child welfare practice, and such studies are feasible only because they employ survival analysis.

Example 3: Evaluating multilevel influences of factors affecting foster care outcome using corrective Cox proportional hazards models. A third level of progress made in child welfare research using survival analysis is the implementation of the corrective Cox proportional hazards model that controls for the clustering effect or autocorrelation. Like conventional statistical models, all survival models assume that study observations in the data set are independent, that is, there is no autocorrelation among the event times (Allison, 1995; Lin, 1994). When this assumption is violated and researchers ignore the violation and use the uncorrected Cox regression in the analysis, the tests of statistical significance are biased, and the bias occurs in ways that cannot be predicted beforehand. The autocorrelation problem is likely to be present in child welfare data. For example, foster care data may include children from the same family who exit or reenter foster care at roughly the same time. Placement of siblings in the same home is mandated by many states or is the preference of many public agencies (Hegar, 1988; Smith, 1996). One study finds that over 70% of sibling pairs are placed together initially and that almost half remain together through the study period (Staff & Fein, 1992). Using the WLW model (i.e., a marginal approach to correct for autocorrelation within the framework of the Cox regression, described in Chapter 6 of this book), Guo and Wells (2003) analyze reunification that controls for sibling group effects and show the importance of being sensitive to the independent-observations assumption and the usefulness of the corrective Cox regression. Autocorrelation may exist in other types of child welfare data, and a corrective strategy is needed whenever researchers aim to test multilevel influences of factors affecting the event durations. Brown (2005) employs the LWA model, another type of marginal approach under the framework of Cox regression, to assess the role of individual-, community-, and agency-level characteristics, particularly their cross-level interactions, in the process of making decisions about placement outcomes.

Example 4: Studying the timing of exit from receipt of Aid to Families with Dependent Children (AFDC) or from receipt of TANF. Survival analysis is widely employed in poverty and welfare-policy research, and perhaps is one of the leading methods suitable for answering research questions concerning welfare dynamics. One such prominent study is Bane and Ellwood (1994), which reveals important findings about lengths of time using AFDC, and factors affecting AFDC dynamics. Many of these findings remained unknown to policy makers and practitioners at the time Bane and Ellwood published their study, and the study became one of the important sources that initiated the debate about pros and cons of welfare reform enacted in the United States in 1996. Bane and Ellwood's work analyzed the 21-year sample of the Panel Study of Income Dynamics (PSID), a longitudinal study that began with a sample of 5,000 families in 1968, by using the discrete-time model of survival analysis (i.e., a method described in Chapter 3 of this book). The central questions the authors pose are these: "How long do female heads with children stay on AFDC? What are the characteristics of those who receive welfare income for relatively long versus short periods of time? How and to what do people leave welfare, and how common is moving from welfare to work?" (Bane & Ellwood, 1994, p. 29). Using survival analysis, the authors found that although the majority of AFDC recipients used the program for a short period of time, a small proportion of recipients used the program for an extremely long period of time. This finding is provocative and motivates researchers and policy makers to think about reasons that welfare does not appear to serve the function of a transitional program and why "dependency on welfare" occurs: "Critical questions arise as to behavior: is long-term use a function of weak incentives to work, of a felt need to stay at home to nurture children, of illness, of a 'culture of poverty' created by welfare 'dependency'? Important value questions arise: is it appropriate for the government to provide an alternative source of support to paid labor market work that allows single parents to stay home, caring for their children?" (Bane & Ellwood, 1994, p. 28). Using the same data as PSID and a similar survival model (i.e., a discrete-time model of multinomial logistic regression that allows the researcher to investigate multiple exit outcomes and competing risks), Harris (1993) found slightly different dynamics of welfare to work: a majority of women work while they are on welfare, more than two-thirds of welfare exits occur through work, and a large family size impedes particularly rapid job exits from welfare. The numerous studies using survival analysis to assess the impacts of welfare reform attest to its popularity in this line of research and illuminate the significance and advantages of using this type of method.

Example 5: Studying family dynamics and the timing of marriage, cohabitation, and dissolution of a relationship. There is a general tendency among Americans to delay marriage. Despite this delay, young people continue to set up households with opposite-sex partners. In fact, most of the decline in numbers of people married by age 25 in the past few decades is offset by entry into cohabitation, and the recent decline in rates of entry into remarriage are fully compensated for by increasing rates of cohabitation. Cohabitation is now the modal path of entry into marriage (Brown, 2000). How do cohabiting couples make decisions about their relationships, and what factors affect the timing of cohabiting couples to marry, to separate, or to remain together? Social work practitioners working with families, couples, and children are concerned with this question because the instability of family dynamics exerts adverse consequences on fragile populations, such as women, minorities, and children. Survival analysis is the dominant approach applied in this area (Brown, 2000; Lichter, Qian, & Mellott, 2006; Lopoo & Western, 2005; Osborne, Manning, & Smock, 2004) and has proven to be robust and effective.

Example 6: Assessing treatment effectiveness in evaluations of mental health service programs. Survival analysis is an efficient tool widely employed in program evaluation, particularly in evaluating mental health services, substance abuse treatment services, and psychiatric service programs. Using the Kaplan-Meier product limit method (i.e., an approach described in Chapter 2 of this book), in conjunction with propensity score matching that is designed to correct for selection bias induced by observational data, Guo, Barth, and Gibbons (2006) reveal that substance abuse treatment is associated with a greater risk of continued involvement of families with child welfare services. Taking another example, Guo, Biegel, Johnsen, and Dyches (2001) confirmed that community-based mobile crisis services resulted in a lower rate of hospitalization than hospital-based interventions, a study that employed the Cox regression. Although mobile crisis services were widely considered to be an integral part of an effective emergency mental health service system, and the modern concept of mobile crisis services was about a quarter century old by the beginning of the twenty-first century, little effort had been directed to formal evaluation of such programs until the study by Guo et al. using effective survival modeling.

This book assumes that readers have knowledge about multiple regression analysis and logistic regression and that they understand basic matrix algebra. However, it has been written in such a way that readers can skip some technical or mathematical expositions without loss of understanding about important concepts and application principles. The book is organized as follows. Chapter 2 highlights key concepts of survival analysis and reviews univariate and bivariate approaches to time-to-event data. Chapters 3 to 5 review three multivariate approaches: the discrete-time models, the Cox proportional hazards model, and parametric models. Among the three, the Cox proportional hazards model is the most important and widely applied approach. Chapter 6 reviews recent advances in survival analysis, namely, the approaches designed to handle multivariate failure time data and that allow researchers to perform a multilevel survival analysis. Chapter 7 reviews computing procedures offered by popular software packages (i.e., SAS, SPSS, and Stata) for conducting survival analysis. Chapter 8 provides concluding remarks.

2

Key Concepts and Descriptive Approaches

This chapter reviews key concepts of survival analysis, two descriptive methods (i.e., the life-table approach and the Kaplan-Meier estimate of survivor function), and graphic approaches. Methods described in this chapter are typically employed at the beginning stage of a quantitative inquiry of time-to-event data, although almost all concepts described in this chapter are important in understanding the entire survival analysis method.

KEY CONCEPTS

1. Censoring

As noted earlier, censoring is the fundamental concept distinguishing survival analysis from conventional statistical methods. So what is censoring? Censoring refers to data incompletion. It occurs when exact event times are known for only a portion of the study subjects, and the remainder of the event times is known only to exceed (or to be less than) a certain value.

There are three basic forms of censoring: right-hand censoring, left-hand censoring, and random censoring. Recall Figure 1.1, the length of time using TANF for a hypothetical example of seven TANF recipients. *Right-hand censoring* refers to the situation in which the ending point of a "spell" or episode is unknown, or the event of interest has not yet occurred at the end of data collection. Suppose we define our study window as 12 months; subject F is right-hand censored because at the ending point of collecting time-to-event data within 12 months, the event of exiting from TANF had not occurred for the subject. The only information known to us is that the ending point of the actual spell for this subject is greater than 12 months. Likewise, if we define our study window as 6 months, then subjects A, B, E, and F are right-hand censored, and the only information known to us is that these subjects' length of time for the event to occur is greater than 6 months.

Left-hand censoring refers to the situation in which the origin or the starting point of a spell is unknown. Consider recipient G who did not remember exactly when she had started to use TANF; however, recipient G had a child 14 months old, so the researcher knew that her length of time using TANF could not be greater than 14 months, because having a dependent child is a requirement for being eligible to receive TANF. In this case, all we know about the length of time G has used TANF is *fewer than* 14 months; therefore, the length of using TANF for G is left-hand censored at 14 months.

In *random censoring,* the researcher observes both the origin and ending points, but the observation is terminated for reasons other than the event of interest. For instance, in a 12-month study window, we observed both the starting and ending points for recipients B and D, but the termination of the two observations was not because the two cases exited from the TANF roll but because they moved to other states. In other words, the observed lengths of time are not exactly the true times of using TANF. Both subjects may or may not continue to use TANF in other states. In this case, the length of time for B and D within a 12-month study window is random censored. Notice that if our study window is shortened to 6 months, then only D is random censored.

A comment about random censoring is warranted. In a child welfare study, foster children may exit foster care for different reasons, or they may accomplish different outcomes: some of them exit foster care because they reunify with their biological parents, some exit because they are adopted by adoptive families, some exit because they join guardianship, and some exit because they reach age 18 and are emancipated from foster care. Random censoring refers to any of these events (or reasons) that is different from the event of interest defined by the study. In a study defining reunification as the event of interest, a termination of foster care that is not due to reunification with the biological family (i.e., termination due to any of the three other reasons: adoption, guardianship, emancipation) is defined as random censoring. Likewise, if a study defines guardianship as the event of interest, then termination due to reunification, adoption, or emancipation is randomly censored.

Standard survival methods can only handle right-hand censoring and random censoring, though the parametric models described in Chapter 5 can accommodate analysis of data with left-hand censoring. Therefore, a common practice in most social behavioral applications of survival analysis is to exclude subjects with left-hand censoring from the analysis.

Statistical analysis following the tradition of Fisher (1935/1971) often assumes a mechanism of randomization under certain contexts (Guo & Fraser, 2010). This is also true for random censoring. Precisely, researchers should assume that *random censoring is noninformative*; that is, the censoring mechanism is under the researcher's control and is out of the study subject's control. When random censoring is under the study subject's control, it then would appear to have patterns among the event times; that is, there would be a systematic difference between the probability of having the defined event and the probability of being censored. When this happens, we call it *informative random censoring*. To understand the violation of the assumption about noninformative random censoring, consider the following hypothetical examples. Suppose four subjects dropped out of a study on relapse of alcoholics. If these subjects drop out because of moving to other cities and the change of residential places is not related to the study, these four subjects are considered a case of noninformative random censoring. If they drop out because they start drinking again and stop notifying investigators of their whereabouts (i.e., censoring is under the study subjects' control), then these subjects are considered a case of informative random censoring. In a study of length of time Ph. D. students take to complete their degree, if the researcher has good reason to suspect that those who drop out of the study are among those who would take a longer time to finish the degree, then these students' random censoring is informative. In a study of length of time subjects remain in marriage, if the researcher has information to believe that those who drop out of the study are more likely to get divorced, then the censoring is informative. For more discussion about the nature and examples of informative random censoring, readers are referred to Allison (1995) and Singer and Willett (2003).

Almost all models of survival analysis assume noninformative random censoring. Violation of this assumption leads to serious bias in model estimation. Unfortunately, no formal test has been developed to detect the violation, and the problem of informative censoring is relatively intractable. Allison (1995, pp. 249–252), however, suggests a procedure of sensitivity analysis that allows analysts to check whether the noninformative random censoring is tenable in a given study based on the analysis model.

The above three forms of censoring are most common in social behavioral data. There are other terms used in the typology of censoring, such as *Type I* and *Type II censoring* (Allison, 1995), or other forms of censuring such as *interval censoring* (Collett, 1994; Hosmer & Lemeshow, 1999). For simplicity of exposition, I do not discuss these issues in this book; readers who are interested in definition and analytic procedures about these types of censoring may find details in the aforementioned references.

2. Dependent Variable, Origin of Time, and Study Window

A typical survival analysis begins with data management. That is, the analyst uses existing data to create the dependent variable. As mentioned earlier, the dependent variable of survival analysis comprises two pieces of information: one is the continuous variable showing the length of time a subject takes to experience the change (i.e., a change from the time origin to experiencing the event or to becoming right-hand censored, and the variable is measured in a metric of days, months, quarters, or years), and the other is a dichotomous variable indicating censoring status.

Figure 1.1 is a graphic representation of study time (also known as analysis time) *after the data management.* A noteworthy feature of the graph is that all study times are standardized to a common origin of time, or time zero. Typically, the raw data do not look like that shown in Figure 1.1. The lengths of time for different study subjects are most likely to appear at different calendar times. Panel A of Figure 2.1 shows the same event histories for the seven hypothetical TANF recipients but is more representative of the real data the analyst has at hand. Specifically, all recipients did not start to use TANF at exactly the same time. Thus, the first data management the analyst conducts is to standardize the time origin, or to make all subjects' starting time zero. Next, the analyst deletes subjects who do not meet the requirement for eligibility of current analysis from the study, such as deleting recipient G (i.e., the left-hand censored subject) from the data set. And finally, based on the definition of the study window, the analyst calculates and creates the duration variable and censoring code. The final data ready for survival analysis after data management look more like Panel B of Figure 2.1. Note that in this figure, subject G is no longer included, and all durations are standardized to a common origin or time 0.

The conversion from Panel A to Panel B in Figure 2.1 is referred to as a conversion of patient time to study time by biostatistician (Collett, 1994), which is an important work of data management. To do this the analyst typically employs data-management functions offered by a software package to create the two variables defining the dependent variable. The simplest case scenario is that there are only two variables indicating starting and ending dates of an event, and both variables are coded in a date format (day/month/year, or other types). The analyst then needs to use time functions in programming (such as *YRMODA* in SPSS) to create the duration variable, and use additional variable(s) indicating reason for exit and the definition of the study window (i.e., 12 months or 6 months) to create the censoring code. Table 2.1 exhibits the input variables (i.e., starting date, ending date, and reason for exit) and output variables after data management (i.e., duration and censoring code) to illustrate the above process. Note that the randomly censored subjects (B and D) and the right-hand censored subject F all have a value 1 on the censoring code, suggesting that the data management treats random censoring the same as right-hand censoring.

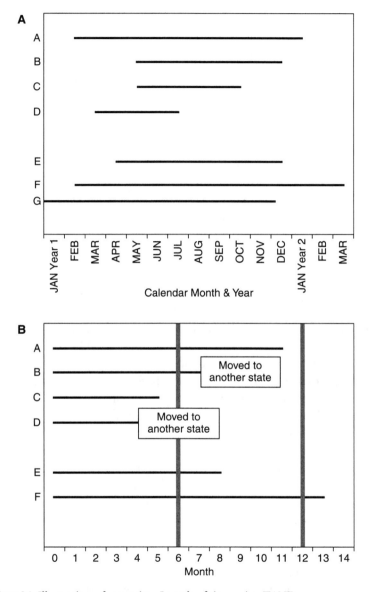

Figure 2.1 Illustration of censoring: Length of time using TANF.

31

Table 2.1 Exhibit of the Input Variables and the Creation of Dependent Variable

ID	Starting Date	Ending Date	Reason for Exit	Duration (Months)	Censoring Code
A	FEB/Year 1	JAN/Year 2	Exit from using TANF	11	0
B	MAY/Year 1	DEC/Year 1	Move to another State	7	1
C	MAY/Year 1	OCT/Year 1	Exit from using TANF	5	0
D	MAR/Year 1	JUL/Year 1	Move to another State	4	1
E	APR/Year 1	DEC/Year 1	Exit from using TANF	8	0
F	FEB/Year 1	MAR/Year 2	Exit from using TANF	13	1

Note: TANF = Temporary Assistance for Needy Families.

The actual data management could be more complicated than the above scenario, in which I use only the simplest scenario of two date variables and one reason-of-exit variable. In practice, the analyst is likely to use more information to create the dependent variable, depending on the structure of input data and the nature of data generation (i.e., administrative data or survey data). In any case, in this process researchers should exercise caution to examine all information available to the study and carefully check the resultant duration and censoring code to ensure the accuracy of data management. It is usually a cumbersome and complex process if one employs multiwave panel data to create the dependent variable. In such cases, what the analyst does is actually a reconstruction of event history for each subject from retrospective information across all waves, and therefore, one must examine several variables across all study waves to see whether the event occurs for each study subject.

Note that different software packages use different conventions to specify censoring or event codes in the analysis. Since event occurrence means that the observed duration is not censored, the analyst needs to specify different values between packages. For instance, SAS uses a *censoring code*, so a subject who is censored should have a value 1 on the censoring code, and a subject who is not censored (equivalently, the duration for this subject indicates event occurrence) should have a value

0 on the censoring code. In contrast, SPSS and Stata use an *event code* that has just the opposite value of a censoring code. Under SPSS/Stata, the analyst should use value 1 to indicate event occurrence, and value 0 to indicate censoring. Using the same data set in different packages, the analyst must be careful about what value the package requires and specify such value carefully. Taking the hypothetical data as an example, suppose a censoring code named CENSOR is created for the six subjects as follows: CENSOR = 1 if the subject is randomly censored or right-hand censored; and CENSOR = 0 otherwise. When running SAS, the analyst specifies CENSOR(1) to indicate that the variable CENSOR is the censoring code and value 1 indicates censoring. When running SPSS or Stata, the analysis can still use the same variable CENSOR but should specify a different value, because SPSS and Stata require knowing which variable and value indicate event occurrence. Since event occurrence is just the opposite of not being censored, the analyst should specify CENSOR(0) in SPSS/Stata.

Defining a study's origin of time and standardizing such origin as time 0 require deliberation. The origin of study time in many research contexts is not as clear as it appears. For instance, a biomedical study may define the onset of a disease as the origin of time. In practice, however, the researcher typically uses the time of diagnosis of the disease as time 0 because the exact onset of disease is difficult to define and to operationalize. Allison (1995) suggests that researchers use the following three rules to choose the origin of time: *(a)* choose a time origin that marks the onset of continuous exposure to risk of having the event—using this rule, one may argue that diagnosis of disease signifies the onset of treatment, although it does not represent the true onset of disease; *(b)* choose the time of being randomly assigned to the treatment condition as the time origin for experimental studies—a time point that logically indicates the onset of an intervention; and *(c)* choose the time that has the strongest effect on experiencing the change under study—that is, among several possible origins, the researcher should choose one that is most sensitive to the risk or likelihood of having the event.

Closely related to the choice of time origin is the decision to define the length of the study window. A study window standardizes the time period within which the researcher observes the change. In any given study, some subjects take a long time to experience the change, and some take a short time to do so. It is an important research question to understand characteristics (i.e., explanatory variables that are statistically significant) associated with subjects who take different times to experience the change. To make such an investigation valid, the analyst must give all study subjects an equal chance (or equal baseline risk) of having the event. Although survival analysis focuses on change rate (i.e., hazard rate) rather than the proportion of subjects who experienced the change, the decision about the study window affects whether the estimated hazard rates are meaningful. To some extent, the decision about the study window is arbitrary, but such an arbitrary decision affects the findings. Suppose that none of the TANF recipients in a study sample exits the program within 3 months; then a study window of 3 months would not allow observance of any occurrence of event within 3 months, and therefore, 100% of the study subjects would be censored. In such a context, the hazard rate is the same for all study subjects and the results about change are not meaningful. In the other extreme, if the study window is too long, that is, if only one recipient out of a sample of 1,000 subjects used the TANF program for 60 months, then a study window of 60 months makes 99.9% subjects uncensored; and therefore, results of the estimated change rate from this study are not comparable to studies using a shorter study window. The decision about a study window is also determined by the convention other researchers use in the substantive area, and by research questions. For instance, child welfare researchers often employ 12 months to study foster care outcomes because federal law requires making permanent arrangements for foster children within 12 months. If a new study aims to compare the change rate of accomplishing reunification in a specific sample to prior studies that use a 12-month window, then a shorter or longer window (i.e., either a 6-month or 18-month window) is not appropriate. In short, researchers should carefully choose a study window by looking into the length of window employed by prior studies, the nature of the research questions, and the type of available data. And more frequently, the final decision is made on a basis of balancing all these factors.

3. Important Functions Describing a Survival Distribution

The study times of all subjects from a sample form a distribution, known as a survival distribution. Using statistics to reveal characteristics of a survival distribution is the fundamental task of survival analysis. Biostatisticians have developed important functions to characterize survival distributions and have derived rigorous theories to show relationships among these functions. Although different distributions may have different parameters, the relationships among these functions remain the same. In this subsection, I review important functions, which serve as building blocks for the entire survival analysis.

Hazard Function. The most important function of survival analysis is the hazard function or hazard rate. Formally, the hazard function is an instantaneous probability measuring rate of change. It can be expressed as a ratio of conditional probability for the event to occur within an extremely small time interval (i.e., when the time interval approaches zero or is infinitesimal) over the time interval, as follows:

$$h(t) = \lim_{dt \to 0} \frac{\Pr\{t \leq T < t + dt | T \geq t\}}{dt}$$

The numerator of this ratio is the conditional probability of having the event at time $t + dt$; that is, given that the event has not yet occurred at time t (equivalently, the study time T is greater than t), what is the probability of having the event in the time interval of $t + dt$? The instantaneous probability further defines such a ratio as a limit, that is, a quantity when dt approaches infinitesimal. By this definition, the hazard function $h(t)$ measures rate of change at time t. Unlike probability defined in other contexts, hazard rates can exceed value 1. Note that in survival analysis, the researcher is interested in length of study time T. A hazard function formally converts duration T to rate of change at time t. Under this definition, a long duration T is associated with a small value of hazard rate $h(t)$ because it takes a long time to make a change and the change rate is slow; and likewise, a short duration T is associated with a large value of hazard rate $h(t)$ because it takes a short time to make a change and the change rate is fast. Hazard function is a formal way to represent change and can be interpreted as speed of change.

Probability Density Function (PDF). This is a popular statistic measuring a distribution, commonly known as a frequency distribution.

Denoted as $f(t)$, a PDF is similar to $h(t)$ but the numerator of the formula is an unconditional probability:

$$f(t) = \lim_{dt \to 0} = \frac{\Pr\{t \leq T < t + dt\}}{dt}.$$

Distribution Function or Cumulative Distribution Function (CDF). This is another popular statistic measuring a distribution. Denoted as $F(t)$, a CDF informs the probability that length of time T is less than or equal to any given value t. It is a definite integral of PDF, from time 0 (i.e., the onset of risk) to time t:

$$F(t) = \Pr\{T \leq t\} = \int_0^t f(u)du.$$

Survivor Function. Having defined hazard function $h(t)$, PDF $f(t)$, and CDF $F(t)$, we now are able to define another important function of survival analysis, that is, the survivor function $S(t)$.[1] It measures the probability of not having the event (surviving to, or remaining in the subject set of having no event) by time t:

$$S(t) = \Pr\{T \geq t\} = 1 - F(t)$$

The label of "survivor" sounds strange, but it is analogous to a subject whose event of interest has not yet occurred at a given time point. Remember that survival analysis originates from studies of mortality, in which context the event of interest is death, and therefore, subjects who have not had the event are survivors. Thus, we use survivor function to measure the probability of not having had the defined event by time t.

The Integrated Hazard Function or Cumulative Hazard Function. The cumulative hazard function is the total number of subjects who would be expected to have the event up until time t. Denoted as $H(t)$, the cumulative hazard is a definitive integral of the hazard function $h(t)$, from time 0 (i.e., the onset of risk) to time t:

$$H(t) = \int_0^t h(u)du.$$

The above functions (i.e., the hazard function $h(t)$, PDF $f(t)$, CDF $F(t)$, survivor function $S(t)$, and the cumulative hazard function $H(t)$)

are equivalent ways to describe a continuous probability distribution. Biostatisticians have proved certain relationships among these functions. The most important relationship is that one can express $h(t)$ as a function of $f(t)$, $S(t)$, $F(f)$, and $H(t)$. Precisely, the following relationships exist:

$$h(t) = \frac{f(t)}{S(T)} = \frac{f(t)}{1 - F(t)} = -\frac{d}{dt}\{\log S(t)\}.$$

The relationship between S(t) and H(t) is as follows: $S(t) = \exp\{-H(t)\}$ or $H(t) = -\log S(t)$.

The above functions are formal ways to describe a survival distribution depicted by a given sample. Researchers use these functions to describe sample data; conduct univariate, bivariate, and multivariate analysis; and draw statistical inferences of survival distribution in the population from which the sample is drawn. Putting them together, what do empirical researchers really need to know about these functions? In this regard, at least the following four issues are important.

First, the most frequently encountered functions are $h(t)$ and $S(t)$. We use these functions to describe change rate at a given time t and the total number of subjects who do not have the event at a given time t. The basic idea of estimating $h(t)$ and $S(t)$ comes from the life-table method, the oldest approach to time-to-event data, dating back to 1662. In a life table, the time intervals are large and discrete, but in the above discussion, we define these functions by treating the increment of time t as infinitesimal (i.e., $dt - > 0$); and therefore, the timing of change is rigorously and precisely treated as a continuous variable. The Kaplan-Meier method is another important approach, and even more popular than the life-table method, for estimating the survivor function $S(t)$, though the method does not estimate the hazard function $h(t)$. Using either method, researchers can perform a univariate analysis to describe sample survival distribution or perform a bivariate analysis to compare survival distributions between groups and discern whether differences observed from the sample on the survival distribution between groups are statistically significant.

Second, a discrete-time model (i.e., the method described in Chapter 3) employs the probability of having the defined event in

person-time data to approximate the hazard rate. The purpose of conducting a discrete-time model is the same as for other multivariate
models (i.e., the Cox proportional hazards model and parametric
models), but it uses probability as a proxy for the hazard rate.

Third, most functions discussed above can be plotted in a graph that
uses study time as the horizontal axis. The purpose of employing graphic
approaches in survival analysis is twofold: one is to describe a sample
survival distribution (i.e., to conduct a univariate analysis) or to compare survival distributions between groups (i.e., to conduct a bivariate
analysis); and the second purpose is to evaluate the nature of the sample
survival distribution and to discern whether certain assumptions
embedded in a specific model are appropriate. These graphic approaches
will be reviewed shortly in this chapter.

Finally, when an estimation method or model does not have
specific parameters (i.e., mathematically derived unknown quantities
in the population) to describe the survival distribution, we call the
method a *nonparametric method*. Examples of nonparametric
methods include the life-table method, the Kaplan-Meier estimation,
and the discrete-time model. When a model does explicitly use parameters to describe the survival distribution (i.e., the distribution is
known to have additional parameters other than $h(t)$, $f(t)$, $F(t)$, $S(t)$,
or $H(t)$, and these additional parameters are called *shape* and *scale*
parameters), we call the modeling process a *parametric method*.
Examples of the parametric method include the Weibull, exponential,
log-normal, log-logistic models, and more. I will review some of these
models in Chapter 5. When a model makes assumptions about the
hazard rate but does not use additional parameters to describe the
distribution of survival times, we refer to the method as a *semipara-*
metric method. An example of the semiparametric method is the Cox
regression. Because no parameters are required to describe the distribution, which is often unknown, the semiparametric models are
also called *distribution-free* models. This feature is one of the advantages offered by the Cox regression and explains why the model is so
popular among survival analysts. With a distribution-free model, the
researchers do not have to make strong and restrictive assumptions
about the survival distribution under study and may apply the Cox
regression anyway. I will review this type of distribution-free model in
Chapter 4.

THE LIFE-TABLE METHOD

A life table is an extension of the traditional frequency table that displays survival functions such as the estimated hazard function and estimated survivor function for individual-level or aggregate data. Although life tables can be constructed on individual-level data, the method is typically employed with aggregate data.

A typical life table based on aggregate data is shown in Table 2.2. This table uses hypothetical data depicting foster children's experience of exiting foster care to achieve family reunification within a study window of 12 months. A total of 310 children comprise the sample. The life table first groups the sample subjects by using a monthly interval. Hence, a total of 13 time intervals appears in the table. The lower bound of the time interval is inclusive, and the upper bound is exclusive. For instance, the very first time interval of the table is [0, 1), meaning that this interval shows survival experience for study children within a time interval bounded by exactly 0 month and less than 1 month. All 310 children enter in the first interval, as no event of reunification occurs at the beginning of the study window or time 0. The column labeled "number entering this interval" simply shows the total number of study subjects who enter the interval, which forms the basis, but not exactly the same number, of risk set for calculating the hazard rate. The column labeled "number failed" indicates the number of subjects who

Table 2.2 Exhibit of the Construction of a Life Table

Interval (Lower, Upper)	Number Entering This Interval	Number Failed	Number Censored	Effective Sample Size	Conditional Probability of Failure	Survivor	Hazard	
0, 1	310	11	14	303	0.0363	1.0000	0.036975	
1, 2	285	6	24	273	0.0220	0.9637	0.022222	
2, 3	255	10	24	243	0.0412	0.9425	0.042017	=11/{[310-(11+14)]+.5(11+14)}
3, 4	221	11	8	217	0.0507	0.9037	0.052009	
...								
12, +	126	0	126	63	0	0.7022	.	=6/{[285-(6+24)]+.5(6+24)}

=0+126/2=63

=285-.5(24)

=5/273

=11/303

=(1-.0363)*1

=310-.5(14)

=(1-.0220)*.9637

Always = 1.0000 for the beginning interval.

=11/{[221-(11+8)]+.5(11+8)}

have the event within this interval. Note that the term "failed" is synonymous with "event occurred"; in survival analysis, just like the term "died," failed or failure is a special terminology indicating event occurrence. There are 11 children who reunified within the very first month. The column labeled "number censored" indicates the number of subjects who are censored; for the very first interval, 14 children are censored. The life-table method assumes that all failures and censorings occur exactly at the midpoint of the time interval. With this assumption, the life table then calculates survivor and hazard functions, along with additional statistics such as "effective sample size" and "conditional probability of failure." The exact formula and illustration of the calculation of these statistics are shown below.

1. Effective sample size is the number of subjects who had not yet failed at the start of the interval. The formula for calculating statistics in this column is effective sample size = number entering − .5(number censored); for the last interval: effective sample size = number failed + .5(number censored). To illustrate, Table 2.2 shows that for the interval [0,1), effective sample size = 310 − .5(14) = 303; and for the last interval [12+), effective sample size = 0 + .5(126) = 63.

2. Conditional probability of failure is an estimate of probability that a subject fails in the interval, given that he or she has not yet failed at the start of the interval. The formula for calculating statistics in this column is conditional probability of failure = (number failed)/effective sample size). To illustrate, Table 2.2 shows that for the interval [0,1), conditional probability of failure = 11/303 = .0363.

3. Survivor function is the probability of not having the event at a time greater than or equal to the starting point of the interval among all study subjects. The formula for calculating statistics in this column is survivor function = (1 − conditional probability of the previous interval) × (survivor function of the previous interval); and the survivor function is constrained to be value 1.0000 for the first interval, meaning all subjects survive to, and hence do not have the event at, the beginning of the study. To illustrate, Table 2.2 shows that for the interval [0,1), the survivor function is 1.0000; for the interval [1,2), the survivor function = (1 − .0363) × 1.0000 = .9637; and for the interval [2,3), the survivor function = (1 − .0220) × .9637 = .9425.

4. Hazard function is an estimate of hazard function (or the rate of change) at the midpoint of the interval. The formula for calculating statistics in this column is number failed/{[number entering − (number failed + number censored)] + .5 (number failed + number censored)}. To illustrate, Table 2.2 shows that for the interval [0,1), the hazard function is 11/{[310 − (11 + 14)] + .5 (11 + 14)} = .036975; and for the interval [3,4), the hazard function is 11/{221 − (11 + 8) + .5(11 + 8)} = .052009. The calculation of hazard function is worthy of explanation. Two important features distinguish the survival analysis from conventional calculation of probability. First, the denominator of the formula is the risk set that serves as a base for calculating the instantaneous probability. Note that the risk set takes number of censored subjects into consideration; it does not throw away the information known to the researcher about the number of censored subjects. And additionally, the denominator is the total number of subjects entering the interval minus half the subjects who either have the event or are censored in the interval. This sophistication in approximating hazard function started from the very first life table established in 1662 and signified the birth of a new branch of statistical analysis (i.e., the survival analysis) that carefully takes censoring into consideration and estimates rate of change for the time-to-event data. This is a seminal contribution made by John Graunt, and it has been followed and refined by biostatisticians since then.

Different software packages may present the life table in a slightly different fashion. For instance, SAS does not show the column of "number entering this interval," but the user can calculate it as .5(number censored) + effective sample size. Almost all packages also offer estimation of standard error (S.E.) associated with a survivor function, which permits a statistical test of the research hypothesis about difference in survivor functions between groups. Since this topic is similar to that depicting the calculation of S.E. for survivor function estimated by the Kaplan-Meier approach, I will describe it in the next section.

What are the primary functions offered by the life table? How useful is a table like this? First, the life table is a descriptive tool for time-to-event data containing censored failure times. The analyst can use a life table to obtain an estimate of median survivor time, which is the time that divides the sample into two halves, such that 50% of sample subjects survive to, or do not have the event by, this time point; and 50% of the sample subjects exit the system or have the event before this time point. In this example, it happens that a median survivor time is not applicable because 70.22% of the subjects survive to the last time interval. Under this condition, a descriptive statistic equivalent to the median survivor time called a quantile can be used instead. For instance, the survivor function for the time interval [1,2) is .9637 and for the time interval [2,3) is .9425. Hence, we know that the 95th percentile of the survivor function is between 2 and 3 months. For this sample, 5% of the children achieved family reunification before approximately 2.5 months, and another 95% took more than 2.5 months to have the event or be censored. As noted earlier, because of censoring, the median defined by conventional statistics cannot be employed in the time-to-event data. Suppose that in another data set, an analyst obtains a "median survivor time" of 5.49 months; this suggests that 50% of the sample subjects take 5.49 months or less to have the event, and another 50% take more than 5.49 months to have the event or be censored.

Second, the life table offers a practical means for comparing survivor functions by group—a first bivariate test of the hypothesis about group differences. Suppose the estimated median survivor time for achieving reunification from an empirical sample for African American children is 5.49 months, and that for non-African American children is 3.00 months. With these estimated statistics, the researcher knows that African American children take a longer time and hence are more difficult than other children to reunify. Using additional statistics such as S.E. associated with the median times, the analyst can further perform a significance test to determine to what extent the observed difference is statistically significant.

Third, the life table permits researchers to gauge the nature of hazard function before running a multivariate model. Many parametric models assume certain types of hazard function, and the choices include a constant hazard rate over time, a piecewise constant hazard rate, and more. A life table, in conjunction with the plot of hazard function over time, provides important information that helps the analyst to choose an appropriate parametric model.

Last, the analyst can use the estimated survivor functions to predict the likelihood of having the event in the future, given that the event has not yet occurred at a given time. Specifically, one can predict the probability of having the event n months later, given that the event has not yet occurred at the start of time interval i, by applying the following equation:

$$P(T > i + n | T > i) = \frac{S_{i+n}}{S_i}.$$

To illustrate, I take a numerical example as follows: knowing that 3 months after entry into foster care, David has not yet reunified, what is the probability that he will remain in care for another 6 months (i.e., or remain in foster care exactly at the beginning of the interval starting with $3 + 6 = 9$ months)? To answer this question, we need to check the survivor functions from a life table suitable to David's experience. Suppose we find from such a table that the survivor function for the interval $[3,4) = .9037$, and the survival function for the interval $[9,10) = .7757$. Applying the above equation, we find that

$$P = \frac{S_{i+n}}{S_i} = \frac{.7757}{.9037} = .8584.$$

Or it's 85.84% likely that David will remain in care for another 6 months, and his chance of reunifying between month 3 and month 9 is $1 - .8584 = .1416$ or 14.2%.

THE KAPLAN-MEIER ESTIMATE OF SURVIVOR FUNCTION

Also known as the *product-limit* estimator, the Kaplan-Meier estimate of survivor function is more popular than the life-table method and is the dominant approach to estimating survivor function among biomedical researchers. This estimator incorporates information from all the observations available, both uncensored and censored, by considering survival to any point in time as a series of steps defined by the observed survival and censored times. Greenwood's formula estimating the variance (hence the standard error) of survivor function allows analysts to compare survival distributions between groups to conduct a significance test. The Greenwood approach is based on a first-order Taylor series expansion (Hosmer & Lemeshow, 1999).

Table 2.3 exhibits the estimation method of the Kaplan-Meier approach with an illustrating data set. Suppose in a child welfare study,

Table 2.3 Exhibit of the Kaplan-Meier Estimate of the Survivor Function

Lengths of time (in months) staying in foster home for a sample of 14 children (* indicates censoring):
1 3* 3* 5 6 7* 7* 8 8 9 10* 12 12* 12*
Estimated Survivor Function and Its 95% Confidence Interval:

Time Interval$_j$	n_j	d_j	$[1-(d_j/n_j)]$	$\hat{S}(t)$	S.E. $\{\hat{S}(t)\}$	95% C.I.	
[0,1)	14	0	1.0000	1.0000	0.0000		
[1,5)	14	1	0.9286	0.9286	0.0688	0.7937	1.0000*
[5,6)	11	1	0.9091	0.8442	0.1019	0.6443	1.0000*
[5,8)	10	1	0.9000	0.7597	0.1218	0.5210	0.9984
[8,9)	7	2	0.7143	0.5427	0.1562	0.2365	0.8488
[9,12)	5	1	0.8000	0.4341	0.1582	0.1240	0.7443
[12+)	3	1	0.6667	0.2894	0.1584	0.0000*	0.5999

* This value is forced to be the maximum of upper bound 1.0000 or the minimum of the lower bound 0.000 because the estimated value is greater than 1.0000 or less than 0.0000.

a researcher observed the lengths of time staying in foster home for a hypothetical sample of 14 children within a 12-month period. Of the 14 children, 7 are censored and their lengths of time are labeled with *. Like the life-table method, the Kaplan-Meier estimator creates a series of time intervals first, but the intervals are formed in such a way that each interval is only for subjects who have the event within the time interval. By this definition, censored subjects do not contribute to the creation of time intervals in the table. This is the case for subjects who are censored, for instance, at month 3 and month 7.

The Kaplan-Meier method begins by sorting the event times in an ascending order and creating time intervals in such a way that each interval j contains only subjects who have event times in the interval. Let n_j denote the number of subjects entering interval j, and d_j denote the number of events occurring within j. The table shows that, initially, all 14 subject enter time interval [0,1); since no event occurs in this interval, $d_j = 0$. All 14 subjects then enter the second interval [1, 5) and n_j remains 14. Since one subject exited foster care within this interval, d_j for [1, 5) = 1. Note how the Kaplan-Meier approach handles the censored subjects. Although censored subjects do not contribute to the formation of time intervals, their information is not thrown away. The number of censored subjects affects the value of n_j for each j. Taking the time interval $[5,6)$ as an example, we see that of the 14 children, 1 has an event time of 1 month, 2 have censored times of 3 months; therefore, by the beginning of month 5 there are $14 - (1+2) = 11$ subjects who enter the interval $[5,6)$, which makes $n_j = 11$ for this interval. The remaining entries for the columns n_j and d_j can be calculated in a similar fashion.

The most important estimates of the Kaplan-Meier method are the estimated survivor function $\hat{S}(t)$, its standard error $S.E.\{\hat{S}(t)\}$, and the estimated 95% confidence interval of $\hat{S}(t)$. $\left[1 - \frac{d_j}{n_j}\right]$ is an intermediate statistic useful for estimating $\hat{S}(t)$. The formulas for calculating all these statistics are shown below with numeric illustrations.

1. The calculation of the intermediate statistic is simply $\left[1 - \frac{d_j}{n_j}\right]$. That is, for the interval $[1, 5)$, $\left[1 - \frac{d_j}{n_j}\right] = \left[1 - \frac{1}{14}\right] = .9286$, and for the interval $[5, 6)$, $\left[1 - \frac{d_j}{n_j}\right] = \left[1 - \frac{1}{11}\right] = .9091$, and so on.

2. The Kaplan-Meier estimate of survivor function for each j can be obtained by using the following equation:

$$\hat{S}(t) = \prod_{j:t_j \leq t}\left[1 - \frac{d_j}{n_j}\right].$$

For instance, for the interval $[5,6)$, $\hat{S}(t) = \prod_{j:t_j \leq t}\left[1 - \frac{d_j}{n_j}\right] = 1 \times .9286 \times$ $.9091 = .8442$; and for the interval $[8,9)$, $\hat{S}(t) = \prod_{j:t_j \leq t}\left[1 - \frac{d_j}{n_j}\right] = 1 \times$ $.9286 \times .9091 \times .9000 \times .7143 = .5427$.

Note that the above calculation (i.e., multiplication of multiple survival probabilities) gives the method its label of product-limit estimator.

3. The Greenwood formulas for calculating the variance and standard error of $\hat{S}(t)$ are as follows:

$$S.E.\left\{\hat{S}(t)\right\} \approx [\hat{S}(t)]\left\{\sum_{j=1}^{k} \frac{d_j}{n_j(n_j - d_j)}\right\}^{1/2}.$$

$$\text{var}\left\{\hat{S}(t)\right\} \approx [\hat{S}(t)]^2 \sum_{j=1}^{k} \frac{d_j}{n_j(n_j - d_j)}.$$

By definition, $S.E.\{\hat{S}(t)\}$ is the square root of $Var\{\hat{S}(t)\}$. For the interval [5,6), the calculation of $S.E.\{\hat{S}(t)\}$ is

$$S.E.\left\{\hat{S}(t)\right\} \approx [\hat{S}(t)] \left\{\sum_{j=1}^{k} \frac{d_j}{n_j(n_j - d_j)}\right\}^{1/2}$$

$$= .8442 \sqrt{0 + \frac{1}{14(14-1)} + \frac{1}{11(11-1)}} = .1019.$$

And finally,

4. The calculation of the 95% confidence interval of the estimated $\hat{S}(t)$ is as follows: $\hat{S}(t) + 1.96 \times S.E.\{\hat{S}(t)\}$. For the interval [5,6), the lower bound of the 95% confidence interval is $.8442 - 1.96(.1019) = .6443$, and the upper bound of the confidence interval is $.8442 + 1.96(.1019) = 1.043$. Since the confidence interval should not exceed a value of 1.0000, we constrained the estimated upper bound to be 1.0000.

The analyst can use the Kaplan-Meier estimate of survivor function in several ways. First, all utilities of estimated survivor functions provided by the life-table method remain valid in the current context. The analyst can use the Kaplan-Meier method to obtain the median survivor time (i.e., the 50th percentile of the survivor function) or other quantiles such as a 90th percentile or 75th percentile of the survivor function. A 95% confidence interval for each of these quantiles can be further attached.

Second, the analyst can employ the estimated $\hat{S}(t)$ and its estimated standard error to perform a significance test about group difference. Doing so, the analyst basically tests a research hypothesis of "H_1: the survivor functions between two groups are not equal" versus the null hypothesis of "H_0: there is no difference in the survivor functions between two groups." The following significance tests are developed based on Greenwood's estimate of the standard error of $\hat{S}(t)$: the log-rank test, the Wilcoxon test, the Breslow test, and the Tarone-Ware test. Most software packages provide results of one or more of these tests. For each test, if the analyst sets up a significance level of $\alpha = .05$, and if the observed p-value of a test is less than .05, then the analyst can reject H_0. The analyst then concludes that the difference in the survivor functions between groups is statistically significant. If the observed p-value is greater than .05, then the analyst fails to reject the null hypothesis and concludes that the difference in the survivor functions between groups is not statistically significant. Computing packages usually use the log-rank test as a default. Among different tests, which one should the analyst use to draw a final conclusion? Collett (1994, pp. 44–45) describes issues that need to be considered when different tests lead to different conclusions. For instance, Collett suggests that when the proportional hazard assumption seems valid (i.e., when observed survivor functions do not cross in the survivor plot), the log-rank test is more appropriate. We will discuss this assumption in detail in Chapter 4.

GRAPHIC APPROACHES

The estimated survivor function $\hat{S}(t)$ and hazard function $\hat{h}(t)$ from the life-table method and the estimated survivor function $\hat{S}(t)$ from the Kaplan-Meier method can be further plotted to produce graphics. In these graphics, each estimated statistic is used as the vertical axis, and the study time is used as the horizontal axis. Based on equations about the cumulative hazard function $\hat{H}(t) = -\log \hat{S}(t)$, the analyst can further produce a cumulative hazard plot or "log-log survivor plot." Most software packages provide graphic functions to facilitate this job. Graphic approaches may be employed to accomplish two goals.

The first goal of using graphics is to have a visual representation of the change process, so that the shape of study subjects' survival distribution, hazard rate, and differences on these functions between groups can be visually examined. The presentation of graphics is a supplement to univariate and bivariate statistics but provides an effective, efficient, and succinct presentation of study results.

The second goal for using graphics is to check tenability of assumptions embedded in multivariate models so that the researcher can gauge whether applying a specific model is appropriate. The researcher may employ the plot of cumulative hazard function (also known as the Nelson-Aalen cumulative hazard plot), or a "log-log survivor plot" (i.e., a plot defining $log[-log S(t)]$ as the vertical axis, and $log\ t$ as the horizontal axis),[2] or a plot of survivor functions $\hat{S}(t)$ for several groups to check whether the hazard rate increases with time, whether there is sufficient evidence to suggest that the survival distribution follows a certain type of parametric model, or whether the proportionality assumption embedded in the Cox regression is valid. These methods will be illustrated in Chapters 4 and 5.

AN ILLUSTRATING EXAMPLE

This section presents an example to show the application of descriptive approaches described in this chapter. The example comes from a larger study investigating the impact of welfare reform on reunification by using three entry cohorts of children who received foster care services prior to and after welfare reform (Wells & Guo, 2003, 2004, 2006). To distinguish the current study, which basically aims to illustrate methodology of survival analysis, from the original study, I used an 80% random sample of the larger study. This example is used for methodological illustration throughout the book.

The substantive interest of this study is to investigate whether children placed in foster care prior to welfare reform return home more quickly than do children placed in foster care after reform. The study grew out of a concern that welfare reform would have a negative effect on families involved in the child welfare system or families at high risk of such involvement. It also examines whether specific factors such as a child's mother's loss of cash assistance show a stronger relationship to the speed with which a child returns home after reform than before.

This study employed a staggered prospective multiple-cohort design. Three entry cohorts of study children (n = 1,278) receiving foster care services in Cuyahoga, Ohio, comprise the sample: children of the prereform cohort entered foster care between 10/1/1995 and 3/31/1996, children of the first postreform cohort entered care between 10/1/1998 and 3/31/1999, and children of the second postreform cohort entered care between 10/1/2000 and 3/1/2001. The staggered prospective multiple-cohort design disentangles the period effect, such as the policy impact of welfare reform, from the cohort effect. With this design, we are able to test the research hypothesis that children placed in foster care prior to welfare reform return home more quickly than do children placed in foster care after reform.

In addition to the entry-cohort variable, the study employs the following explanatory variables: child age at entry (grouped as 0, 1–3, 4–7, 8–11, and 12–16), gender, race (grouped as African American and others), reason for placement (categorized as physical abuse, neglect, dependency, and other), first placement type (categorized as kinship care, foster care, and other), mother's income from TANF and wages (operationalized as total monthly average income prior to child's exit from foster care), and percentage of mother's income from wages (operationalized as the proportion of mother's total income from wages prior to child's exit from foster care).

We impose a study window of 12 months. That is, regardless of the point at which the child entered foster care during the recruitment period of October 1 to March 31, we follow each child for 12 months to see whether the study event occurred within the 12-month period. If the event occurred, then the child is coded as noncensored; if the event did not occur by the end of a 12-month period, then the child is coded as censored (i.e., a type of right-hand censoring). The primary event of interest for this study is reunification with family. By this definition, all other types of exits from the foster care within 12 months, such as exits due to guardianship or adoption, are coded as censored (i.e., a type of random censoring). In Chapter 3, I will use this example to illustrate survival analysis of multiple exits, at which place I'll introduce additional events of interest. Because of censoring and the time-to-event nature of data, we chose to use survival analysis as a primary analytic method for this study.

Like other quantitative research, the first task of a survival analysis is to conduct univariate and bivariate analyses. Table 2.4 presents results of these analyses. The column headed "% or M(SD)" presents descriptive statistics of explanatory variables. These statistics are produced by conventional methods for descriptive analysis; that is, the column shows percentage distribution for categorical variables, and mean (standard deviation) for continuous variables. These statistics allow us to examine distributional patterns of the explanatory variables.

The primary interest lies in the univariate and bivariate analysis of the dependent variable: child's length of time in foster care prior to

Table 2.4 Example of the Impact of Welfare Reform on Reunification—Sample Descriptive Statistics and 90th Percentile of Survivor Function Estimated by the Kaplan-Meier Method

Variable	% or M(SD)	The 90th Percentile of the Survivor Function
Entry cohort		
Prereform	24.3%	3.06
Postreform 1	33.0%	5.29
Postreform 2	42.7%	6.28
Child age at entry		
0	27.6%	6.47*
1–3	19.5%	4.83*
4–7	20.2%	6.14*
8–11	17.2%	3.45*
12–16	3.0%	4.14*
Child gender		
Male	49.9%	5.52
Female	50.1%	4.50
Child race		
African American	74.7%	5.98*
Other	25.3%	3.78*
Reason for placement		
Physical abuse	11.2%	2.60***
Neglect	65.6%	5.91***
Dependency	13.5%	5.26***
Other	9.7%	4.70***
First placement type		
Kinship	49.5%	4.86
Foster	42.6%	4.90
Other	7.9%	5.91
Mother's income from TANF & wages		
(Total monthly average prior to exit)	312.53 (465.72)	
$0–299	66.6%	7.98***
$300–999	25.7%	3.22***
$1000–1999	6.0%	5.29***
$\geq$ $2000	1.6%	0.23***
% mother's income from wages (prior to exit)	49.05 (45.99)	

continued

Table 2.4 (Continued)

0%–24.9%	45.4%	4.11
25%–49.9%	5.2%	6.54
50%–74.9%	5.6%	3.91
75%–100%	43.9%	6.47

$^*p < .05$, $^{**} p < .01$, $^{***} p < .001$, Breslow (Generalized Wilcoxon) Test.
Note: % or M(SD) = percentage distribution for categorical variables, and mean (standard deviation) for continuous variables.

reunification with censoring. To fulfill this goal, I ran the Kaplan-Meier estimation of survivor curve for the whole sample, and ran the same analysis for each study variable. I employed the Breslow test to determine whether differences on survivor functions between groups are statistically significant. I plotted survivor curves based on the Kaplan-Meier estimation as well as hazard curves. Note that the hazard functions were not estimated by the Kaplan-Meier estimation. Running *SAS Proc Lifetest*, the hazard function is estimated by the life-table method. Running *Stata sts graph, hazard*, the hazard function is also estimated by the life-table method, but the hazard curve is further smoothed by additional procedures within Stata.

Because more than 50% of the study children were still in foster care by the end of the 12-month window, the median survivor function is not meaningful. In other words, the only information we know from the data is that the median is greater than 12 months. Therefore, I chose the 90th percentile of the survivor function as a replacement for the median. As shown by the third column of Table 2.4, the 90th percentiles of the survivor function for the three cohorts are as follows: 3.06 months for the prereform cohort (ec = 1), 5.29 months for the first postreform cohort (ec = 2), and 6.28 months for the second postreform cohort (ec = 3). The 90th percentile survivor function can be interpreted as the length of time it takes for 10% of the study children to reunify. Thus, for instance, it takes 3.06 months for 10% of the prereform cohort to achieve reunification. The bivairate analysis confirms the direction of the welfare-reform impact on reunification hypothesized by the study; that is, children placed in foster care prior to welfare reform return home more quickly than do children placed in foster care after reform. However, the Breslow test shows that the differences in survivor functions among the three cohorts are not statistically significant. There are many reasons that this finding is not statistically significant. Among other things, the current investigation is bivariate and does not control for other covariates. We need to conduct further analysis, particularly multivariate modeling, to test the research hypothesis.

Figure 2.2 shows two survivor plots: Panel A was produced by *SAS Proc Lifetest*, and Panel B was produced by *Stata sts graph*. The survivor curve shows that at the beginning of the study window or time 0, all study children (100%) are in foster care and no event (reunification with family) occurs for any child. As the study (analysis) time goes by, the proportion of children remaining in foster care gradually decreases. Of the three survivor curves being compared, the curve on the top indicates the slowest speed of change, and the curve on the bottom indicates the fastest speed of change. The plot shows a clear pattern—that is, at most time points, the proportion of children remaining in foster care for the second postreform cohort (ec = 3) is the highest, the proportion remaining in care for the first postreform cohort (ec = 2) is the second highest, and the proportion remaining in care for the prereform cohort (ec = 1) is the lowest. Thus, the plot indicates that foster children who entered foster care after welfare reform reunify at a slower speed than those who entered care before welfare reform. Again, the differences are not statistically significant using a bivariate test, and it's important to test the differences using a multivariate model.

Figure 2.3 presents hazard plots produced by SAS and Stata. Notice that a high value of hazard function at a specific time point indicates a fast speed of change at that time. The hazard plot shows a similar pattern as that of the survivor plot, though it also indicates that the change rate is not constant over the 12-month period. The most important message the hazard plot conveys is that the prereform cohort tends to have high hazards in the earlier period (i.e., around month 2), while the two postreform cohorts tend to have high hazard rates in the later period of the study window (i.e., after month 8) and accelerate the speed after that. This pattern is more clearly shown by the smoothed plot (i.e., Panel B).

The bivariate analysis (Table 2.4) reveals other important predictors of a fast reunification. In general, older children reunified at a faster speed than younger children ($p < .05$ from the Breslow test); African American children had more difficulty in reunifying than other children ($p < .05$); children placed because of physical abuse reunified at a faster speed than other children ($p < .001$); and most important, income (i.e., both cash

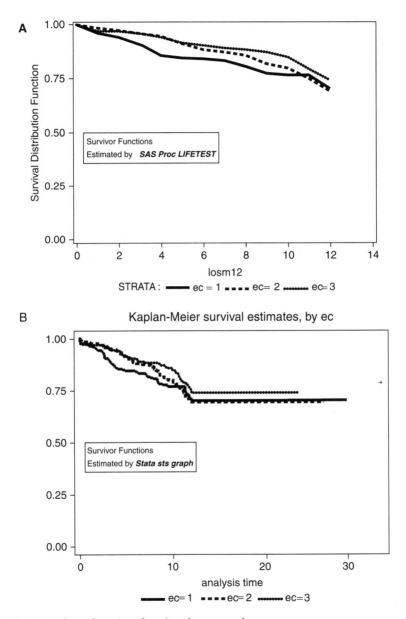

Figure 2.2 Plots of survivor functions by entry cohort.

A

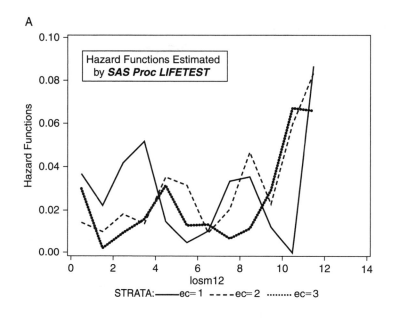

B

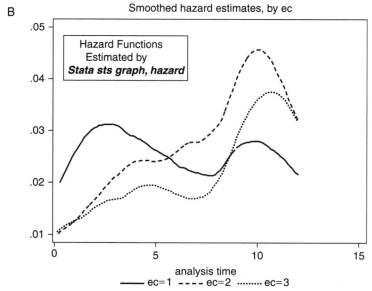

Figure 2.3 Plots of hazard functions by entry cohort.

assistance and wages) matters—children whose mothers had a total monthly average income of more than $2,000 had the fastest speed of reunifying; and the impact of income on reunification speed is probably nonlinear because the 90th percentiles for the four groups of children whose mothers fall into different income categories change in a nonlinear fashion ($p < .001$). To some extent, the bivariate test partially confirms the second research hypothesis proposed by the study, that is, a child's mother's loss of cash assistance impacts the speed of reunification.

Additional survivor and hazard plots could be produced for this study; it would be especially worthwhile to examine these functions for variables that are statistically significant. I did not do this work for simplicity of presentation.

3

The Discrete-Time Models

This chapter reviews the first type of multivariate model analyzing time-to-event data: the discrete-time models. The primary feature of this type of model is its approximation of hazard rate by using probability estimated from a person-time data set. When the study focuses on a single event, the analyst uses a binary logistic regression to estimate the probability. When the study focuses on multiple events (i.e., termination of study time due to more than one reason), the analyst uses a multinomial logit regression to estimate multiple probabilities. The discrete-time model of multiple events is also known as competing-risks analysis. In this chapter, I first provide an overview of the discrete-time models. Next I describe data conversion and the binary logistic regression for analyzing a single event. And finally I review issues related to data conversion and the multinomial logit model for analyzing multiple events.

OVERVIEW

The basic idea of discrete-time modeling is simple: applying a logit model to a well-defined data set that pools together individuals' event histories, using probability of event occurrence based on such data as a proxy of hazard rate, and then estimating regression coefficients of predictor variables on the probability of event occurrence. The discrete-time model was developed by Paul Allison (1982). According to Allison (1995, pp. 211–212), in a discrete-time model, "each individual's history is broken down into a set of discrete time units that are treated as distinct observations. After pooling these observations, the next step is to estimate a binary regression model predicting whether an event did or did not occur in each time unit."

Why and when do we need to apply this method? In general, most analyses suitable to the Cox regression can be implemented with discrete-time models. The advantage of using this method is that the procedure is simply an extension of running logistic regression and is easy for users to apply. The model offers an effective approach to handling time-varying covariates—a central task for most studies using longitudinal data.

The disadvantage is that as a discrete-time model, it uses week, month, quarter, or year as a time unit; as such, it measures change rate in a coarse manner and inevitably causes the study to lose information. For instance, in a discrete-time model using month as a unit, a subject with event time of 1 day is treated the same as another whose length of time is 30 days. This does not seem to be a serious problem for longitudinal data collected from a multiwave panel study, or for studies in which the event times are not truly measured as a continuous variable, or for event times that are not sensitive to the coarseness of time metric. When any of these issues becomes a concern, however, the analyst may consider using a continuous-time model such as the Cox regression or a parametric model.

A comment on the differences and similarities between probability and hazard rate is warranted. Probability commonly quantifies the scale of uncertainty and informs the researcher as to the extent an event of interest occurs out of a given risk set. As such, it measures likelihood of event occurrence within a narrowly defined time segment—or is more applicable to cross-sectional data. A hazard rate measures rate of change and is more applicable to longitudinal data. Hazard rate is also a probability, but is a special type of probability. Known as an instantaneous probability, the hazard rate measures the probability limit when the time increment approaches infinitesimal. In general, the two concepts cannot and should not be confused. Only under well-defined contexts, such as in discrete-time modeling when researchers have converted individual-level data to person-time data, can the two concepts be used interchangeably.

Indeed, using probability as a proxy of hazard rate is an innovative contribution by Allison that simplifies complicated research issues.

Hence, the key to discrete-time modeling is to create a well-defined data set. Precisely, the modeling process involves the following steps: *(a)* define the event of interest, a study window, a unit of time interval, and censoring; *(b)* convert person data into person-time data; and *(c)* run a binary logistic regression (or a multinomial logit model, if analyzing multiple events) based on the person-time data. The first step has been discussed in Chapter 2, so in the following discussion, I focus on steps 2 and 3.

CONVERTING PERSON DATA INTO PERSON-TIME DATA

Most data sets in social work research are organized as person-level data. That is, in such data sets, each study subject contributes one and only one data line. The discrete-time model should be applied to person-time data. Thus, the first work the analyst conducts is converting person data into person-time data.

The conversion involves several steps. First, based on the study time, the analyst creates multiple data lines for each study subject based on the definitions of the study window, the time interval, and censoring. Suppose a study defines 1 year as a study window and a quarter as a discrete time unit. Then a person whose study time is 1 year contributes four data lines to the person-time file, a person whose study time is 2 quarters contributes two data lines, and so on.

Next, the analyst codes the dependent variable of the logistic regression for the time-person data. The coding should follow the information about the study time and the censoring code originally observed in the person-level data. In a binary logistic regression, the dependent variable is typically dichotomous, such that $Y = 1$, if the event occurs, and $Y = 2$ otherwise. The coding values are arbitrary, and the analyst can always specify the value indicating event occurrence when running the logistic regression. In this text, I choose to use values 1 and 2, and use 1 to indicate event occurrence. The discrete-time model gives an event-occurrence code only to the person-time at which the event occurs. Thus, if a person has a study time of 1 year (i.e., 4 quarters) and contributes four data lines, the dependent variable Y is coded as "no event" or value 2 for the first three data lines, and only for the fourth data line is Y coded as "event" or value 1. Note how the discrete-time model handles censoring. If a subject has a study time of three quarters with a random censoring, then the subject contributes three data lines to the person-time data, and none of the three lines has an "event" code or value 1 for Y. If a subject has a study time of 1 year and the study time is censored at the end of the study window, then the subject contributes four data lines, and none of the four lines has a value 1 for Y. If a subject has a study time of 1 year but actually has the event at the end of the study window (i.e., not censored), then the subject contributes four data lines and only the last data line has an "event" code or value 1 for Y.

Finally, the analyst codes the independent variable of the person-time data. If an independent variable is time fixed (e.g., gender, race, age at entry, etc.), then the same value shown in the person data for a specific subject would appear on all data lines on this variable in the person-time data. A great advantage of using the discrete-time model is its ability to analyze time-varying covariates. A time-varying covariate is also called a time-dependent variable in the literature; and likewise, a time-fixed variable is called a time-constant or time-independent variable. Time-varying covariates are those that may change value over the course of observation. Incorporating time-varying covariates in a study makes the investigation truly dynamic, that is, it looks into the relationship between the dependent variable (i.e., the timing of the event occurrence) and an independent variable from a truly changing perspective. Suppose our data set shows that a study child's mother's average quarterly income changes over a 1-year study window and the child's study time is 4 quarters; the income variable of the person-time data will show different values on the four data lines, with each measuring mother's income in a specific quarter.

To illustrate the data conversion for analyzing a single event, I use the same example presented in Chapter 2. Recall that in this study, I define reunification within 12 months as the event of interest. A child who either terminated the study time for reasons other than reunification or did not reunify by the end of the 12-month window is defined as censored. I also decide to use 2 months as the time interval. I refer to this interval as a bi-monthly interval throughout this chapter. Here I chose a bi-monthly interval as the time metric based on the consideration that a quarter would be too coarse, and a month would be too fine, resulting in person-time data that would be too large. Additionally, prior studies show that staying in foster care less than 2 months is considered

Table 3.1 Exhibit of a Person-Data File (n = 1,278)

Obs	id	losp1	cen_r
1	1	129.00	1
2	2	180.00	0
3	3	1.00	0
. . .			
10	10	258.00	0
11	11	365.25	1
. . .			

Obs: observed data line.
id: identification number.
losp1: length of stay in the first spell of foster care (days).
cen_r: censoring code (1 censored, 0 event reunification).

short term. With a bi-monthly metric, the study can sufficiently distinguish between short-term and long-term placements.

Table 3.1 exhibits a portion of the person-level data, a file representing a typical structure researchers see from common data files. In this data file, I have 1,278 study subjects; hence, each subject has one and only one data line, and there are 1,278 data lines in total. The variable *losp1* is the length of time a child stays in foster care measured in days, and the variable *cen_r* is the censoring code (cen_r = 1, if censored; and cen_r = 0, if the event occurs).

After data conversion, I obtain a person-time data file. A portion of the person-time file is shown in Table 3.2. The variable *reunify* is the dependent variable for the logistic regression: reunify = 1, event occurrence; and reunify = 2, no event. The variable *bm* is a variable indicating the order of the current bi-month, such that 1 signifies the first bi-month, 2 the second, and so on. The variable *black* is a time-fixed variable indicating child race; as such, it does not change values across the data lines for each child.

In this data file, each data line represents "1 person bi-month," and two data lines represent "2 person bi-months." Therefore, "2 person bi-months" could mean two different things: it could mean one person staying in foster care for two bi-months (i.e., 4 months), or two persons each staying for one bi-month (i.e., 2 months).

The 1,278 subjects contribute 6,112 data lines or 6,112 bi-months in total. These 6,112 person bi-months form a risk set for the discrete-time modeling. Timing of reunification within a 12-month study window for

Table 3.2 Exhibit of a Person-Time Data File After Data Conversion (n = 6,112)

Obs	id	losp1	cen_r	black	bm	reunify
1	1	129.00	1	1	1	2
2	1	129.00	1	1	2	2
3	1	129.00	1	1	3	2
4	2	180.00	0	0	1	2
5	2	180.00	0	0	2	2
6	2	180.00	0	0	3	1
7	3	1.00	0	0	1	1
31	10	258.00	0	1	1	2
32	10	258.00	0	1	2	2
33	10	258.00	0	1	3	2
34	10	258.00	0	1	4	2
35	10	258.00	0	1	5	1
36	11	365.25	1	1	1	2
37	11	365.25	1	1	2	2
38	11	365.25	1	1	3	2
39	11	365.25	1	1	4	2
40	11	365.25	1	1	5	2
41	11	365.25	1	1	6	2

reunify 1 = reunified
2 = no
bm Bi-month indicator
black a time-fixed variable.

Limitation of discrete-time: LOS = 1 day is treated same as LOS = 60 days.

Event (reunification) occurred in each of these time-intervals .

1,278 children has transformed to a problem of calculating probability of reunification out of 6,112 bi-monthly exposure times. The probability of reunification based on the person-time data (i.e., the proportion of occurred events out of the risk set of 6,112 person bi-months) is not a hazard rate per se, but a good proxy of a hazard rate.

Note how the person-time file handles censoring and codes events. The first study child (id = 1) stayed in foster care for 129 days ($losp1$ = 129) or more than 4 months; therefore, this subject contributes three data lines (3 bi-months) in the person-time file; since this child's time is censored (cen_r = 1), reunify is coded 2 or no event. Three study subjects (id = 2, 3, and 10, respectively) have noncensored data because their cen_r = 0; hence, all these subjects have an event code ($reunify$ = 1), but the value only applies to their very last data lines.

Note that the subject whose id = 3 stayed in foster care for only 1 day, but this child is treated the same as a child who stayed in foster care for 60 days. This is the limitation of discrete-time modeling due to the coarse time metric noted earlier.

Tables 3.3 and 3.4 illustrate the conversion of a time-varying covariate from person-level data to person-time data for the same study

Table 3.3 Exhibit of Time-Varying Covariates (i.e., Bi-Monthly Welfare Cash Assistance) Shown by a Person-Level Data File (n = 1,278)

Obs	id	bmc1	bmc2	bmc3	bmc4	bmc5	bmc6	losp1	cen_r
1	1	0.00	0.00	0.00	0.00	0.00	0.00	129.00	1
2	2	0.00	0.00	0.00	0.00	0.00	0.00	180.00	0
3	3	322.09	322.09	0.00	0.00	0.00	0.00	1.00	0
...									
10	10	479.41	479.41	472.54	465.66	465.66	465.66	258.00	0
11	11	0.00	0.00	0.00	0.00	0.00	0.00	365.25	1
...									

Obs: observed data line.
id: identification number.
bmc1: Dollar amount of cash assistance received in the1st bi-month (i.e., months 1 and 2) with a 2-month lag.
bmc2: Dollar amount of cash assistance received in the 2nd bi-month (i.e., months 3 and 4) with a 2-month lag...
bmc6: Dollar amount of cash assistance received in the 6th bi-month (i.e., months 11 and 12) with lag.

Table 3.4 Exhibit of a Time-Varying Covariate Shown by the Person-Time Data File After Data Conversion (n = 6,112)

Obs	id	bm	reunify	cuse
1	1	1	2	0.00
2	1	2	2	0.00
3	1	3	2	0.00
4	2	1	2	0.00
5	2	2	2	0.00
6	2	3	1	0.00
7	3	1	1	322.09
31	10	1	2	479.41
32	10	2	2	479.41
33	10	3	2	472.54
34	10	4	2	465.66
35	10	5	1	465.66
36	11	1	2	0.00
37	11	2	2	0.00
38	11	3	2	0.00
39	11	4	2	0.00
40	11	5	2	0.00
41	11	6	2	0.00

Obs: observed data line.
id: identification number.
bm: bi-month indicator.
reunify: a binary variable indicating event occurrence.
cuse: A time-varying covariate measuring dollar amount of cash assistance.

sample. Table 3.3 is the person-level file. In this file, variables *bmc1* to *bmc6* are time-varying variables indicating the dollar amount the child's mother received from AFDC cash assistance in each of the 6 bi-months. After the data conversion, all six variables are combined into one variable called *cuse* in the person-time file (see Table 3.4), but the time-varying information appears on different data lines for different children.

The conversion of person data to person-time data requires intensive and careful work of data management. Typically, it requires application of powerful programming functions offered by a computing package. Depending on the nature of the person-level data, programming to fulfill this task may become challenging. Students of survival analysis may use this challenge to strengthen their programming skills and take the opportunity to learn more about a software package. There are good references that show programming commands useful to the data conversion (e.g., Allison, 1995, pp. 212–221, for SAS users; Guo, 1992, for SPSS users; and StataCorp, 2007, pp. 21-22, and Cleves, Gould, and Gutierrez, 2004, for Stata users).

BINARY LOGISTIC REGRESSION

After creating the person-time data, the analyst can run a binary logistic regression on the data set to estimate the discrete-time model. This section reviews statistical principles and application issues pertaining to binary logistic regression. The information can be found in most textbooks dealing with this topic.

Denoting the binary dependent variable as Y_i ($Y_i = 1$, if the event occurs at a specific person-time unit, and $Y_i = 0$, if the event does not occur) for the *i*th unit ($i = 1, \ldots N$), the vector of independent variables as X_i, and the vector of regression parameters as β, a binary logistic regression depicts the probability of event occurrence as follows:

$$P(Y_i|X_i = x_i) = E(Y_i) = \frac{e^{x_i\beta}}{1 + e^{x_i\beta}} = \frac{1}{1 + e^{-x_i\beta}}$$

This is a nonlinear model, meaning that the dependent variable Y_i is not a linear function of the vector of the independent variables x_i. However, by using an appropriate link function such as a logit function, we can express the model as a generalized linear model (McCullaph & Nelder, 1989). A link function in the current context refers to a process of variable transformation. Although Y_i is not a linear function of x_i, its transformed variable through the logit function (i.e., the natural logarithm of odds or $\log\{P(Y_i)/[1-P(Y_i)]\}$) becomes a linear function of x_i:

$$\log_e(\frac{P}{1-P}) = x_i\beta$$

where P denotes $P(Y_i)$.

The logistic regression model is estimated with a maximum likelihood estimator. To ease the exposition, I now assume that there are only two independent variables, x_1 and x_2. The log likelihood function of the logistic regression model with two independent variables can be expressed as follows:

$$\log_e l(\beta_0, \beta_1) = \sum_{i=1}^{n} Y_i(\beta_0 + \beta_1 x_{1i} + \beta_2 x_{2i}) -$$

$$\sum_{i=1}^{n} \log_e[1 + \exp(\beta_0 + \beta_1 x_{1i} + \beta_2 x_{2i})]$$

The partial derivative of $\log \ell$ with respect to β maximizes the likelihood function. In practice, the problems are seldom solved analytically, and we often rely on a numerical procedure to find estimates of β. Long (1997, pp. 56–57) described three numerical estimators: the Newton-Raphson method, the scoring method, and the B-triple-H (BHHH) method. Typically, a numerical method involves the following: (a) insert starting values (i.e., "guesses") of β_0, β_1, and β_2 in the right-hand side of the above equation to obtain a first guess of $\log \ell$; (b) insert a different set of β_0, β_1, and β_2 into the right-hand side equation to obtain a second guess of $\log \ell$; by comparing the new $\log \ell$ with the old one, the analyst knows the direction for trying the next set of β_0, β_1, and β_2; the process from step (a) to step (b) is called an *iteration*; (c) replicate the above process several times (i.e., run several iterations) until the largest value of $\log \ell$ is obtained (i.e., the maximum log likelihood function) or until the difference in $\log \ell$ between two iterations is no longer greater than a predetermined criterion value, such as 0.000001.

Estimated values of β_0, β_1, and β_2 (i.e., $\hat{\beta}_0, \hat{\beta}_1$ and $\hat{\beta}_2$) are logistic regression coefficients at which the likelihood of reproducing sample observations is maximized.

As in running OLS regression or other multivariate models, the analyst must be sensitive to the nature of the data at hand and the possibility of violating assumptions. Routine diagnostic analyses, such as tests of multicollinearity, tests of influential observations, and sensitivity analyses should be used to assess the fit of the final model to the data. A number of statistics have been developed to assess the goodness-of-fit of the model. Details of goodness-of-fit indices for a logistic regression model can be found in textbooks on logistic regression or limited dependent variable analysis (for instance, Kutner, Nachtsheim, & Neter, 2004; Long, 1997). Here I summarize a few indices and include cautionary statements for their use.

1. *Pearson chi-square goodness-of-fit test.* This is a test that detects major departures from a logistic response function. Large values of the test statistic (i.e., those associated with a small or significant p value) indicate that the logistic response function is not appropriate. However, it is important to note that the test is not sensitive to small departures (Kutner et al., 2004).

2. *Chi-square test of all coefficients.* This test is a likelihood ratio test and analogous to the F test for linear regression models. We can perform a chi-square test using the log-likelihood ratio, as follows:

Model Chi-square $= 2$ log-likelihood of the full model

-2 log-likelihood of the model with intercept only

If the Model Chi-square $> \chi^2$ ($1 - \alpha$, df = number of independent variables), then we reject the null hypothesis stating that all coefficients except the intercept are equal to zero. As a test of models estimated by the maximum likelihood approach, a large sample is required to perform the likelihood ratio test and this test is problematic when the sample is small.

3. *Hosmer-Lemeshow goodness-of-fit test.* This test first classifies the sample into small groups (e.g., g groups) and then calculates a test statistic using the Pearson chi-squares from the $2 \times g$ tables of observed and estimated expected frequencies. A test statistic that is less than χ^2 ($1-\alpha$, df = g-2) indicates a good model fit. The Hosmer-Lemeshow test is sensitive to sample size. That

is, in the process of reducing the data through grouping, we may miss an important deviation from fit due to a small number of individual data points. Hence we advocate that before concluding that a model fits you should perform an analysis of the individual residuals and relevant diagnostic statistics (Hosmer & Lemeshow, 1989, p. 144).

4. *Pseudo-R^2*. Because the logistic regression model is estimated by a non-least-squares estimator, the common linear measure of the proportion of the variation in the dependent variable that is explained by the predictor variables (i.e., the coefficient of determination R^2) is not available. However, several pseudo R^2s for logistic regression model have been developed by analogy to the formula defining R^2 for the linear regression model. These pseudo R^2s include Efron's, McFadden's, adjusted McFadden's, Cox and Snell's, Nagelkerke/Cragg and Uhler's, McKelvey and Zavoina's, count R^2, and adjusted count R^2. In general, a higher value in a pseudo R^2 indicates a better fit. However, researchers should be aware of several limitations of pseudo R^2 measures and interpret their findings with caution. UCLA Academic Technology Services (2008) presented a detailed description of each of these pseudo R^2s and concluded:

> Pseudo R-squares cannot be interpreted independently or compared across datasets: they are valid and useful in evaluating multiple models predicting the same outcome on the same dataset. In other words, a pseudo R-squared statistic without context has little meaning. A pseudo R-square only has meaning when compared to another pseudo R-square of the same type. On the same data, predicting the same outcome. In this situation, the higher pseudo R-square indicates which model better predicts the outcome.

AN ILLUSTRATING EXAMPLE OF THE DISCRETE-TIME MODEL ANALYZING A SINGLE EVENT

In this section, I present an illustrating example of the discrete-time model analyzing a single event. The example applies binary logistic regression to person-time data. The data conversion has been discussed in the first section of this chapter. For substantive discussion of the study issues, research questions, and hypotheses, readers may revisit the illustrating example presented in Chapter 2.

Recall that the primary interest of this study is to test the hypothesis that welfare reform creates difficulties for children in reunifying with their families when those families experience material hardship. To test this hypothesis, the study employs two variables to measure material hardship and the impact of welfare reform: one is a time-varying covariate of mother's income from TANF and wages, and the other is the percentage of mother's income from wages. Acknowledging that it takes time for material hardship to have an impact on reunification, the study employs a 2-month lag on the above two variables. Thus, the child's study time is linked to the mother's total income and the percentage of that income from wages at a point 2 months earlier.

Table 3.5 presents the results of the discrete-time model of reunification within 12 months. The model has a good fit to data, as indicated by the model chi-square that is statistically significant. The odds ratio can be interpreted in a conventional fashion as one does for logistic regression. The result does not show significant differences among the three cohorts, though it confirms that children of the postreform cohorts are less likely to reunify than their prereform counterparts: other things being equal, the chance of reunification for children of the second postreform cohort is 21.6% lower than that for children of the prereform cohort (i.e., $(1 - .784) \times 100 = 21.6\%$), and the chance of reunification for children of the first postreform cohort is 7.4% lower than that for children of the first prereform cohort (i.e., $(1 - .926) \times 100 = 7.4\%$).

With regard to the two mother income-related variables, the results indicate that mother's total income from TANF and wages affects the odds of reunification. The results show that other things being equal, every $100 increase in the mother's monthly income 2 months earlier increases the odds of reunification by 4.3% ($p<.01$). The percentage of mother's income due to wages is not statistically significant, though the results show that other things being equal, every 10 percentage point increase in the percentage of income due wages decreases the odds of reunification by 0.1%.

The estimated discrete-time model finds two other important variables that are statistically significant: age at entry ($p<.05$) and reason for placement ($p<.01$, $p<.05$). In general, infants and children who were placed for reasons of neglect or other have the lowest odds for reunification.

Table 3.5 Estimated Discrete-Time Model of Reunification within 12 Months—
A Binary Logistic Regression Based on the Person-Time Data Set

Chapter 3: Binary Logit

Variable	B	Odds Ratio
Entry cohort (prereform)		
Postreform 1	−.077	.926
Postreform 2	−.244	.784
Child age at entry (8–11)		
0	−.419 *	.658
1–3	−.147	.863
4–7	−.287	.751
12–16	−.167	.846
Child gender (male)		
Female	.099	1.105
Child race (other)		
African American	−.214	.807
Reason for placement (physical abuse)		
Neglect	−.725 **	.485
Dependency	−.463 *	.629
Other	−.733**	.480
First placement type (kinship)		
Foster	.173	1.189
Other	−.197	.821
Mother's income from TANF & wages		
(2-month lag, time varying, in $100)	.042 **	1.043
% mother's income due to wages		
(2-months lag, time varying, 10% points)	−.001	.999
Bi-month indicator (6)		
1	−.377 *	.249
2	−.200	.297
3	−.013	.358
4	−.513 **	.217
5	.089	.396
Constant	−2.188	
Model chi-square (df)	141.45 (20)**	
Number of study subjects	1,278	
Number of subject bi-months	6,112	

*$p<.05$, ** $p<.01$.
Reference group is shown in parentheses for a categorical variable.

The estimated model also includes five bi-monthly dummy variables. The model shows that these time variables vary substantially in the 12-month period, and two of them (the first and fifth bi-months) are statistically significant. Results suggest that the probability of reunification at each bi-month is not constant. Thus, if we run a parametric model, an exponential model is probably not appropriate because the exponential model assumes a constant hazard rate throughout the study period, and this data set may have violated this assumption.

DISCRETE-TIME MODEL ANALYZING MULTIPLE EXITS

The discrete-time-multiple-exits model follows a similar procedure as that for the discrete-time-single-exit model. That is, the analyst needs to convert the person-level data into person-time data and then run a multinomial logit model instead of a binary logistic regression using the person-time data. This section highlights issues that are unique to this type of modeling.

The distinguishing feature of the multiple-exits model is that it analyzes more than one exit or event as the events of interest simultaneously. As such, the model allows the analyst to investigate competing risks. In foster care research, children who exit from foster care because of reunification are likely to have quite different determinants from those who exit because of adoption, or because of guardianship, or because of emancipation. The multiple-exits model provides an analytic tool to answer research questions that deal with more than one reason for children exiting the system, and helps to determine how these reasons differ.

Data conversion for the multiple-exits model is the same as for the single-exit model, except that the analyst needs to code multiple values for the dependent variable of the multinomial logit model.

To illustrate, I use the same data as for the previous example but add an exit outcome, "guardianship." In the previous example, the event of interest was reunification; in this context, if a child exits foster care due to guardianship, then the child's event time is censored. In the current context, I use two events to define exit outcomes—guardianship and reunification—and treat all other types of exit, such as adoption or moving to other states, as random censoring.

Specifically, the coding scheme for the dependent variable is as follows: the dependent variable *event* = 1, if the child's study time is not censored and the exit outcome is reunification; *event* = 2, if the child's study time is not censored and the exit outcome is guardianship; and *event* = 3, if the child's study time is right-hand censored or randomly censored. Table 3.6 shows a portion of the person-time data for the multiple-exits model, which was converted from person-level data.

A multinomial logit model uses the probability of having outcome $Y = k$ ($k = 1, 2, \ldots K\text{-}1$) as the dependent variable and can be expressed as follows:

$$P_k(Y_i = k | x_i) = \frac{\exp(\beta_k' x_i)}{\displaystyle\sum_{k=1}^{K} \exp(\beta_k' x_i)}$$

where the vector of independent variables is denoted as x_i, and the vector of regression parameters for the kth outcome is denoted as

Table 3.6 Exhibit of a Person-Time Data File with Multiple Exits

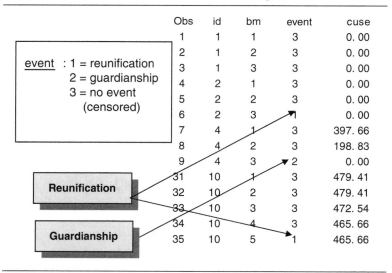

	Obs	id	bm	event	cuse
	1	1	1	3	0. 00
	2	1	2	3	0. 00
event : 1 = reunification	3	1	3	3	0. 00
2 = guardianship	4	2	1	3	0. 00
3 = no event	5	2	2	3	0. 00
(censored)	6	2	3	1	0. 00
	7	4	1	3	397. 66
	8	4	2	3	198. 83
	9	4	3	2	0. 00
	31	10	1	3	479. 41
Reunification	32	10	2	3	479. 41
	33	10	3	3	472. 54
	34	10	4	3	465. 66
Guardianship	35	10	5	1	465. 66

Obs: observed data line.
id: identification number.
bm: bi-month indicator.
event: dependent variable indicating occurrence of events or censoring.
cuse: A time-varying covariate measuring dollar amount of cash assistance.

Table 3.7 Estimated Discrete-Time Model of Multiple Exits (Reunification and Guardianship) within 12 Months—A Multinomial Logit Model Based on the Person-Time Data Set

Chapter 3: Multiple Exits - Multinomial Logit Model

Variable	Reunification Odds Ratio	Guardianship Odds Ratio
Entry cohort (prereform)		
Postreform 1	0.930	0.674*
Postreform 2	0.786	0.352**
Child age at entry (8−11)		
0	0.652*	1.513
1−3	0.866	1.058
4−7	0.743	0.935
12−16	0.848	1.010
Child gender (male)		
Female	1.112	1.139
Child race (other)		
African American	0.789	0.815
Reason for placement (physical abuse)		
Neglect	0.491**	1.166
Dependency	0.634*	1.342
Other	0.479**	1.244
First placement type (kinship)		
Foster	1.119	0.211**
Other	0.783	0.049**
Mother's income from TANF & wages		
(2-month lag, time varying, in $100)	1.050**	1.003
% mother's income due to wages		
(2-months lag, time varying, 10% points)	0.966	0.917**
Bi-month indicator (continuous variable)	1.305**	1.137**
Likelihood ratio	3328	
Number of study subjects	1,278	
Number of subject bi-months	6,112	

$^{*}p < .05$, $^{**}p < .01$.
Reference group is shown in parentheses for categorical variables.

β_k. Choosing category K as a reference group (i.e., $\beta_K = 0$), we can express log odds or *logit* as a linear function of the vector of independent variables as

$$\log \frac{P_k(x_i)}{P_K(x_i)} = \beta'_k x_i, \mathrm{k} = 1, \ldots, \mathrm{K} - 1.$$

Note that in this model, a separate parameter vector β_k is estimated for each $K–1$ logit. Thus, if you have K outcomes, the model estimates K–1 sets of regression coefficients.

Analysts may assess the fit of a multinomial logit mode in a similar fashion as for a binary logistic regression and interpret the odds ratio as they do for a binary model.

Table 3.7 presents results of the estimated discrete-time model examining reunification and guardianship. A test based on the estimated model likelihood ratio indicates that the model has a decent fit to data. Results show that clearly, the odds of reunification and the odds of guardianship are indeed associated with different sets of determinants. For reunification, the significant explanatory variables are age ($p<.05$), reason for placement ($p<.01$, $p<.05$), mother's income from TANF and wages ($p<.01$), and the bi-month indicator. For guardianship, the significant explanatory variables are entry cohort ($p<.05$, $p<.01$), first placement type ($p<.01$), percentage of mother's income due to wages ($p<.01$), and the bi-month indicator ($p<.01$). The results in general confirm the research hypothesis, that is, children who entered foster care after welfare reform are less likely to join guardians than their prereform counterparts, an increase in mother's income from TANF and wages improves the likelihood of family reunification, and an increase in the percentage of mother's income due to wages decreases the likelihood of the child joining guardians. And finally, the model shows that the hazard rate of either family reunification or joining guardians is not constant over the study period.

For additional application examples of the discrete-time-multiple-exits model, readers are referred to Harris (1993) and Shook (1999).

4

The Cox Proportional Hazards Model

T his chapter describes the Cox proportional hazards model (also known as Cox regression). The model was first proposed by Sir David Cox in his famous paper "Regression Models and Life Tables" in 1972. Cox regression is one of the most important developments in contemporary statistics. His paper is the most highly cited journal article in the entire literature of statistics (Allison, 1995).

THE PROPORTIONAL HAZARDS MODEL AND THE PARTIAL LIKELIHOOD METHOD

There are several reasons that the Cox regression is so important and widely applied in biomedical, engineering, economic, social, and behavioral sciences. First, prior to the Cox regression, the leading approach to multivariate survival analysis was the parametric model, which requires the analyst to know the nature of the survival distribution being studied and to be sure the chosen model does not violate assumptions embedded in certain types of parametric distributions. The Cox regression is a distribution-free model and does not require such information. Second, the main estimation method Cox developed is *partial likelihood*, which is innovative in several ways. Among other things, it allows the user to estimate the regression coefficients of the proportional hazards model without having to specify the baseline hazard function (again, it is a distribution-free approach), and the estimates depend only on the *ranks* of the event times, not their numerical values. Because the model depends only on ranks, any monotonic transformation of the event times will leave the coefficient estimates unchanged. Third, the Cox regression is the very first model that permits the user to incorporate the time-varying covariates in survival analysis. The parametric model cannot incorporate time-varying covariates; the discrete-time model allows users to do this job, but the method was developed after Cox's work. And fourth, with appropriate specifications, the Cox regression can be employed to answer challenging research questions. Innovative models based on the Cox regression include competing risks analysis, the nonproportional hazards model, creation of time-varying covariates that allow a time-fixed covariate to interact with event time, and more.

The proportional hazard model can be expressed as

$$h_i(t) = h_0(t)\exp(\beta_1 x_{i1} + \ldots + \beta_k x_{ik}) \tag{4.1}$$

where $h_i(t)$ is the dependent variable (operationalized as the hazard rate at time t for subject i), x_1 to x_k are k independent variables or covariates, and β_1 to β_k are the regression coefficients; $h_0(t)$ is a baseline hazard function and is left unspecified. The baseline hazard function can be thought of as the hazard function for an individual whose covariates all have values of 0.

The model of (4.1) can be expressed in the following form by taking the logarithm of both sides of the equation:

$$\log h_i(t) = \alpha(t) + \beta_1 x_{i1} + \ldots \beta_k x_{ik}.$$

Two features of the model are worth noting: *(a)* the model dos not require assumptions about the underlying distribution of the survival times (i.e., no matter what the actual form of the survival distribution is—exponential, Weibull, Gompertz, standard gamma, generalized gamma, log-normal, or log-logistic—the analyst can run the same Cox regression model for all); and *(b)* the model assumes a constant ratio of the hazards for any two individuals.

The second feature gives the model its name: proportional hazards model. Because there is no requirement for understanding the underlying survival distribution, and because of the proportional hazards assumption, the model is also known as a *semiparametric* model, to distinguish it from the *parametric* models such as those discussed in Chapter 5, and from the *nonparametric* models such as a life table, Kaplan-Meier estimate, and discrete-time models.

The proportional hazards assumption is that the hazard for any individual in a sample is a fixed proportion of the hazard for any other individual, and the ratio of the two hazards is constant over time. Precisely, it means that in a *log(hazard)* plot, the log(hazard) curves for any two individuals should be *strictly parallel*. What is important here is that with this assumption, $h_0(t)$, the baseline hazard function cancels out from the formula expressing a hazard ratio for any two individuals i and j, as follows:

$$\frac{h_i(t)}{h_j(t)} = \frac{\cancel{h_0}\exp(\beta_1 x_{i1} + ... + \beta_k x_{ik})}{\cancel{h_0}\exp(\beta_1 x_{j1} + ... + \beta_k x_{jk})}$$
$$= \exp[\beta_1(x_{i1} - x_{j1}) + ... + \beta_k(x_{ik} - x_{jk})]$$

Because of this feature, the analyst can estimate β coefficients of the model without having to specify the baseline hazard function $h_0(t)$.

Because $h_0(t)$ cancels out, Cox developed a method called partial likelihood estimation, which discards the baseline function and treats only the second part of the equation [i.e., $\exp(\beta_1 x_{i1} + ... + \beta_k x_{ik})$] as though it were an ordinary likelihood function. He calls this function a "partial likelihood." The estimation method aims to maximize the partial likelihood function.

Understanding how partial likelihood estimation operates is not crucial to applying the Cox regression. However, based on my teaching experiences, I find that this is a great opportunity for students not only to gain a solid grasp of the Cox regression but also to acquire basic knowledge about maximum likelihood—the fundamental estimator of contemporary statistics! Students should not be scared away by maximum likelihood as it is an important method that a serious quantitative researcher in the twenty-first century cannot afford to ignore.

Recall Chapter 3 where I described three steps in maximum likelihood estimation for a binary logistic regression. Basic concepts used in that process, such as the likelihood function to be maximized, starting values, iteration, convergence, and convergence criteria, can be better understood through the following description of the partial likelihood method. My description below follows Allison (1995, pp. 122–126); it assumes no ties in the event times, and there is only one independent variable x used in the model.

All maximum likelihood approaches begin with developing a likelihood function the estimator aims to maximize. So our first task is to develop the partial likelihood function. To do so, let's first sort the data in an ascending order by the study time T, so that the first subject in our sample has the shortest study time or highest hazard rate h_1, the second subject has the next shortest study time or second highest hazard rate h_2, and so on, until the last or the nth subject who has the longest study time or lowest hazard rate h_n. From equation (4.1), the hazard function for the first subject can be expressed as

$$h_1(t) = h_0(t)\exp(\beta x_1)$$

where x_1 denotes the value of x for subject 1. Likewise, we can have a similar expression of hazard functions for all subjects. Taking the sum of hazards over all sample subjects, we obtain a risk set as

$$h_1(t) + h_2(t) + \ldots h_n(t)$$

The likelihood for individual 1 to have the event at time t is simply the ratio of hazard over the risk set, or is the hazard for subject 1 at time t divided by the sum of the hazards for all subjects who are at risk of having the event at time t. That is,

$$
\begin{aligned}
L_1 &= \frac{h_1(t)}{h_1(t) + h_2(t) + \ldots h_n(t)} \\
&= \frac{\cancel{h_0}\exp(\beta x_1)}{\cancel{h_0}\exp(\beta x_1) + \cancel{h_0}\exp(\beta x_2) + \ldots + \cancel{h_0}\exp(\beta x_n)} \\
&= \frac{\exp(\beta x_1)}{\exp(\beta x_1) + \exp(\beta x_2) + \ldots + \exp(\beta x_n)}
\end{aligned}
$$

So the likelihood for subject 1 becomes a partial likelihood. Three important features of the partial likelihood are noteworthy: (a) the baseline hazard is canceled out; (b) as a result, the likelihood function is solely expressed by βx—the coefficient to be estimated and the predictor; and *(c)* the model carefully takes the information of censored cases into account when building the likelihood function—censored cases are not excluded, and their information (i.e., the hazard functions) is built into the construction of the risk set.

Writing the partial likelihoods for each of the n subjects and multiplying all these partial likelihoods together, we obtain the sample partial likelihood:

$$PL = \prod_{i=1}^{n} L_i = L_1 {}^*L_2{}^* \ldots {}^* L_n$$

where each censored subject j has a likelihood of value 1, or $L_j^0 = 1$. Putting together and expressing the individuals' likelihood functions by their βx, we obtain the formal expression of the sample partial likelihood function:

$$PL = \prod_{i=1}^{n} \left[\frac{e^{\beta x_i}}{\sum_{j=1}^{n} Y_{ij} e^{\beta x_i}} \right]^{\delta_i} \qquad (4.2)$$

where $Y_{ij} = 1$ if $t_j > t_i$; and $Y_{ij} = 0$ if $t_j < t_i$. Here Y_{ij} serves as a switcher (i.e., on and off), indicates that the study times are rank ordered, and signifies that the estimating algorithm should not use the information for those whose events occurred at a point earlier than the current i^{th} subject in the calculation of the risk set (i.e., the formation of denominators). This makes sense because those who already had the events have exited the set and are no longer elements of the risk set. In equation (4.2), δ_i is the censoring code and takes the value of 0 or 1. If $\delta_i = 0$ (i.e., the study time is censored), then the whole partial likelihood for this subject equals value 1—that is,

$$L_{(censored)} = \left[\frac{e^{\beta x_i}}{\sum_{j=1}^{n} Y_{ij} e^{\beta x_i}} \right]^{0} = 1,$$

Otherwise, the likelihood takes a non-one value.

It's a convention in statistics to take the logarithm of the likelihood function (i.e., to take the log on both sides of equation (4.2)). Doing so, the *log PL* we seek to maximize becomes

$$\log PL = \sum_{i=1}^{n} \delta_i \left[\beta x_i - \log \left(\sum_{j=1}^{n} Y_{ij} e^{\beta x_j} \right) \right] \tag{4.3}$$

With this log partial likelihood function, the analyst can search for the best estimate of β. The analyst typically inserts a starting value of β into the right-hand side of the equation to obtain a first "guess" of *log PL*. Through several iterations, the analyst finds that further modification of β is no longer necessary because the difference between the current *log PL* and the *log PL* obtained from the previous iteration is less than a predetermined value called the convergence criterion, typically a very small value such as .000001. Then the analyst stops searching, and the β so obtained is the best that maximizes *log PL*. Using this β, the likelihood of reproducing the sample data is maximum or optimal.

To aid in a full understanding of the partial likelihood algorithm, I developed an Excel program using a data set originally published by Collett (1994), but slightly modified by Allison (1995, p. 123). The variable SURV is the study time or survival time in months, beginning with the month of surgery, for 45 breast cancer patients, and the variable DEAD is the event code (DEAD = 1, if died; DEAD = 0, if censored). Table 4.1 shows the Excel program. The electronic version of the Excel sheet can be downloaded from the companion Web page of this book. Readers need to download the program and type a trial value for β into the red cell. The value shown in the blue cell is the *log PL* associated with the β. After a few rounds of trials or iterations, the user obtains the highest or maximized value of *log PL*.

Readers are encouraged to do this exercise. The program provides readers with a visual tool that allows them to have hands-on experience with the maximum likelihood approach. I also encourage readers to pay attention to the setup of the Excel program, that is, pay attention to key Excel functions, and compare the cell functions with equation (4.3). By doing so, they will gain a solid understanding of the Cox regression and its partial likelihood estimator.

Table 4.1 An Excel Program Illustrating the Partial Likelihood Method

SURV	DEAD	X	exp(BX)	(Likelihood)$_i$
5	1	1	2.481839	-3.617331097
8	1	1	2.481839	-3.590109681
10	1	1	2.481839	-3.562126474
13	1	1	2.481839	-3.533337609
18	1	1	2.481839	-3.503695314
23	1	0	1	-4.382147443
24	1	1	2.481839	-3.46057019
25	1	1	2.481839	-3.42865441
26	1	1	2.481839	-3.395686337
31	1	1	2.481839	-3.361594206
35	1	1	2.481839	-3.326298655
40	1	1	2.481839	-3.289711604
41	1	1	2.481839	-3.251734938
47	1	0	1	-4.121258917
48	1	1	2.481839	-3.195901789
50	1	1	2.481839	-3.154110993
59	1	1	2.481839	-3.110497268
61	1	1	2.481839	-3.064894298
68	1	1	2.481839	-3.017111914
69	1	0	1	-3.875931301
70	0	0	1	0
71	1	1	2.481839	-2.924576845
71	0	0	1	0
76	0	1	2.481839	0
100	0	0	1	0
101	0	0	1	0
105	0	1	2.481839	0
107	0	1	2.481839	0
109	0	1	2.481839	0
113	1	1	2.481839	-2.519111737
116	1	1	2.481839	0
118	1	1	2.481839	-2.343493007
143	1	1	2.481839	-2.242576212
148	1	0	1	-3.039320202
154	1	1	2.481839	0
162	0	1	2.481839	0
181	1	0	1	-2.703195624
188	0	1	2.481839	0
198	0	0	1	0
208	0	0	1	0
212	0	0	1	0
212	0	1	2.481839	0
217	0	1	2.481839	0
224	0	0	1	0
225	0	1	2.481839	0

-85.01497806   0.909

=D2*((M2*E2)- LN(SUM(F2:F46)))

= DEAD*[BX- ln(sum(expBX))]

Iteration	B	Log PL	Trial of B
1	1	-85.03106272	Starting value 1
2	2	-86.900471	>1
3	0.5	-85.37631751	<1
4	0.1	-86.52919769	<.5
5	0.7	-85.10597875	>.5
6	0.8	-85.03932324	>.7
7	0.9	-85.01515182	>.8
8	0.95	-85.01824654	>.9
9	0.92	-85.01520404	<.95
10	0.91	-85.01497872	<.92
11	0.908	-85.01498139	<.91
12	0.909	-85.01497806	0.000000659

Criterion=.000001

This spreadsheet program illustrates the calculation of partial likelihood for a Cox model with one predictor. The input data come from "Output 5.4: Survival Times for Breast Cancer Patients" [Allison, (1995), p.123].

Note That There Are No Ties in Survival Times

To use this program, enter your trial value for B into the red cell. You will obtain the partial likelihood function from the blue cell.

-85.01497806

Warning: Always keep these yellow cells empty!!

In practice, researchers seldom have just one independent variable. With more than one independent variable, the estimation of partial likelihood has to employ a numeric approach such as a Newton-Raphson algorithm. To describe this method is beyond the scope of this book. Readers who are interested in this topic may consult Allison (1995, p. 83).

TIES, MODEL FIT, AND DIAGNOSIS

In the above description of the partial likelihood estimator, I assume that study times are not tied. This is certainly not realistic. In practice, two or more subjects may have exactly the same value on study time. When study times are tied, the analyst needs to choose an appropriate method to handle ties.

Several methods have been developed to take care of tied times. The basic idea for all these methods is to consider true *time-ordering* among tied subjects. The Breslow method assumes that the observed ties occurred sequentially, and this method is used as the default in popular software packages (such as SAS). The Exact method considers all possible orderings; that is, if there are five tied times, it considers all possible orderings (i.e., a total of 5! = 120 orderings) to estimate the Cox regression. The Efron method also considers all possible underlying orderings that might exist but uses a numeric approximation to simplify the computations. And the Discrete method assumes that tied times are discrete. For a given study, how does the analyst choose a method to handle ties? Allison (1995, p. 137) summarizes six points to answer this question. In general, the Efron method is highly recommended, although the Exact and Discrete methods also produce good and virtually the same results in many study contexts. In the mid-1990s when Allison wrote his text, computing time was not as fast as it is today; therefore, running time (particularly the time it takes for a large study) was a concern. However, running time should not be a problem with today's fast-speed computers.

Table 4.2 presents the results of the Cox regression for the same illustrating example introduced in Chapter 2. The table compares the results of estimated coefficients and standard errors among three methods handling ties: Breslow, Efron, and Exact. Note that results from the Efron and Exact methods are exactly the same, whereas the estimated coefficients and standard errors estimated by Breslow are slightly different from the other two methods. Given the recommendations provided by the literature, I suggest that users always choose the Efron method.

To determine whether an estimated Cox model fits the data to an acceptable degree, the analyst often performs a model chi-square test. The test is similar to that for a binary logistic regression (see Chapter 3). Basically, it performs a likelihood ratio test to compare −2 log likelihoods between a model with all independent variables and a null model. The test statistic is subject to a chi-square distribution with a given degree of freedom (i.e., the number of independent variables included). A p-value $<.05$ of the test statistic (i.e., the model chi-square, sometime labeled a model Wald chi-square in some packages) indicates a good model fit. Under such a condition, the analyst

Table 4.2 Comparing Results of Estimated Cox Regression Model Among Three Methods for Handling Ties

Chapter 4: Cox - ties

Variable	*Breslow* *B (S.E.)*	*Efron* *B (S.E.)*	*Exact* *B (S.E.)*
Entry cohort (prereform)			
Postreform 1	.0378(.1599)	.0382(.1599)	.0382(.1599)
Postreform 2	−.1174(.1572)	−.1167(.1572)	−.1167(.1572)
Child age at entry (8–11)			
0	−.3770(.1942)	−.3781(.1943)	−.3781(.1943)
1–3	−.0594(.1860)	−.0598(.1860)	−.0598(.1860)
4–7	−.2222(.1828)	−.2226(.1828)	−.2226(.1828)
12–16	−.1132(.1953)	−.1134(.1953)	−.1134(.1953)
Child gender (male)			
Female	.1187(.1171)	.1188(.1171)	.1188(.1171)
Child race (other)			
African American	−.2319(.1303)	−.2323(.1303)	−.2323(.1303)
Reason for placement (physical abuse)			
Neglect	−.5923(,1600)**	−.5941(.1596)**	−.5941(.1596)**
Dependency	−.3344(.2192)	−.3354(.2192)	−.3354(.2192)
Other	−.6451(.2476)**	−.6473(.2476)**	−.6473(.2476)**
First placement type (kinship)			
Foster	.1467(.1279)	.1468(.1279)	.1468(.1279)
Other	−.1872(.2633)	−.1875(.2633)	−.1875(.2633)
Mother's income from TANF & wages (in $100) (Monthly average prior to exit)	.0715(.0105)**	.0716(.0105)**	.0716(.0105)**
% mother's income due to wages (in 10% points) (Monthly average prior to exit)	−.0578(.0155)**	−.0578(.0155)**	−.0578(.0155)**
Model Wald Chi-square (df)	109.50(15)**	109.89(15)**	109.89(15)**

*p<.05, ** p<.01.
Reference group is shown in parentheses for categorical variables.

concludes that the current model can reject the null hypothesis that all the regression coefficients equal zero, and equivalently, at least one coefficient that is not equal to zero. Hence, the model is acceptable.

Diagnosis of the Cox regression refers to checking whether the proportional hazards assumption is tenable for a given data set. That is, it tests whether the ratio of hazard rates for any two study individuals is constant over time. The primary tool to facilitate this test is the log-log survivor plot (i.e., a plot defining $log[-log\,S(t)]$ or $-log[-log\,S(t)]$ as the vertical axis, and $log\,t$ as the horizontal axis, where t denotes study time). See Chapter 2 for more discussion of this plot. Researchers may do the plot by independent variables (say one plot is for a comparison of $log[-log\,S(t)]$ curves between males and females, the second plot is for the comparison of curves among racial groups, and so on). If they find that the plotted lines for a given independent variable are reasonably parallel, then they conclude that the proportional-hazards assumption has not been violated.

It's worth noting that the literature does not provide clear guidelines on the importance of the proportional-hazards assumption to the Cox regression, and what to do if there is evidence suggesting that such an assumption is violated. In early applications of the Cox regression, researchers typically presented the log-log survivor plots to justify their use of the model; and in practice, when researchers found that the assumption was violated in their data set, they were hesitant to apply the model. However, Allison (1995) personally thinks that the concern about the proportionality assumption is often excessive; and whenever a Cox regression includes time-varying covariates, the proportionality assumption is violated. Allison (1995, pp. 154–155) states: "The reason people focus so much attention on the PH assumption is that the model is *named* for that property. At the same time, they often ignore such critical questions as: Are all the relevant covariates included? Is the censoring mechanism noninformative? Is measurement error in the covariates acceptably low? ... It's unlikely that the PH assumption is ever exactly satisfied, but that's true of nearly all statistical assumptions."

TIME-VARYING COVARIATES

Incorporating time-varying covariates into the Cox regression is simple, and most software packages provide programming functions that allow users to specify the variables signifying time varying. Formally, the Cox regression with time-varying covariates can be expressed as

$$\log h_i(t) = \alpha(t) + \beta_1 x_{i1} + \beta_2 x_{i2}(t),$$

where $x_2(t)$ is a covariate that varies in value for each individual with time t. The model indicates that the hazard at time t depends on the value of time-fixed variable x_1, and the value of the time-varying variable x_2 at time t. $x_2(t)$ can be defined using information about the study subjects prior to time t, thereby allowing for lagged or cumulative values of some variables.

Running a Cox regression with time-varying covariates requires programming to inform the software package which variables are time-varying. Computing packages follow different conventions to do the job. For instance, both SAS and SPSS require a single-record data file (also known as a "wide" file, or multivariate file) in which each study subject occupies one data line, and the time-varying information is organized by several variables. Suppose we have a time-varying variable about a child's mother's income at different time points in a 12-month study window. Mother's income is time-varying in the current context. Suppose that a study collects mother's income every other month during the study window; hence the data contain six pieces of income information. A single-record data file organizes the six pieces of income information as six separate variables.

In contrast, Stata requires a multiple-record data file (also known as a "long" file, or univariate file). The distinguishing feature of this type of file is that each study individual occupies one or more data line, depending on the number of time-varying pieces of information available in the data set and the subject's length of study time. Using the same hypothetical case of six pieces of time-varying income information, Stata requires a child having six data lines, if his study time is 12 months; and requires a child having only three data lines, if his study time is 6 months. Stata *stset* is the command to implement data management of this kind.

The key task in modeling the impact of a time-varying covariate on event occurrence is to link the independent variable at a specific time to the study time. The analyst needs to check the user's guide of a software package and follow the rules to specify the Cox regression. The syntax files using SAS and Stata for the illustrating example presented in the next section are available on the companion Web page of this book.

Estimating the partial likelihood for models with time-varying covariates is time consuming. However, this is no longer a problem in today's applications of such models, thanks to the tremendous progress made in computer technology. However, a proportional hazards model with time-varying covariates becomes complex, and researchers should carefully examine the research questions and seek a best strategy to use the time-varying information. There are different ways to use the time-varying information and the best solution may not necessarily be a Cox regression with time-varying covariates. This issue will be revisited in the section discussing application issues.

AN ILLUSTRATING EXAMPLE OF THE COX REGRESSION

To illustrate the application of the Cox regression, I present results of applying the model to the same study used earlier about foster children's timing of reunification within 12 months, where three entry cohorts are compared, and mother's income-related variables are employed. Table 4.3 presents results of the estimated model.

Results show that the reunification model fits the data well, as reflected in the model chi-square of 84.35 (df $= 15$, $p<.000$).

An estimated hazard ratio is simply the exponent of the estimated regression coefficient, and it is a convention among researchers using the Cox regression to present hazard ratios rather than regression coefficients. The model shows that, other things being equal, the hazard of reunification for children who entered foster care at age 0 is only about 66% of the hazard for children who entered care at ages 8–11 ($p<.05$). Alternatively, the hazard ratio can be interpreted as the relative difference in speed of reunification, as, other things being equal, the reunification speed for infants (i.e., those who entered care at age 0) is 34% (i.e., $(1 - .66) \times 100 = 34\%$) slower than that of children who entered care at ages 8–11. For a continuous variable, one may interpret the hazard ratio in a similar fashion. Taking mother's income as an example, the model shows that, other things being equal, for every $100 increase in mother's income from TANF and wages, the hazard of reunification goes up by an estimated 4.1% ($p<.01$). Alternatively, the finding may be interpreted as,

Table 4.3 Estimated Cox Proportional Hazards Model with Time-Varying Covariates

Chapter 4: TV

Variable	Hazard Ratio
Entry cohort (prereform)	
Postreform 1	0.956
Postreform 2	0.825
Child age at entry (8–11)	
0	0.660 *
1–3	0.876
4–7	0.759
12–16	0.876
Child gender (male)	
Female	1.103
Child race (other)	
African American	0.801+
Reason for placement (physical abuse)	
Neglect	0.492 **
Dependency	0.640 *
Other	0.487 **
First placement type (kinship)	
Foster	1.125
Other	0.802
Mother's income from TANF & wages (in $100)	
(Time-varying)	1.041 **
% mother's income due to wages (in 10% points)	
(Time-varying)	0.0978
Model Wald Chi-square (df)	84.35(15)**

+$p<.1$, *$p<.05$, **$p<.01$.
Reference group is shown in parentheses for categorical variables.

other things being equal, every $100 increase in mother's income from TANF and wages increases reunification speed by 4.1%.

Comparing the Cox regression to the discrete-time model (i.e., comparing the current table to Table 3.5), we find that the two models provide almost identical findings. This implies that the substantive findings of this study about significant predictors of reunification speed, the magnitudes of influence of significant predictors, and the importance of mother's income to reunification are strong; and both models are probably appropriate to the study sample, given that the findings are consistent.

APPLICATION ISSUES

This section examines application issues researchers commonly encounter in projects that employ the Cox proportional hazards model. To become a skillful user of the Cox regression, the analyst needs to be cautious about the type and nature of research questions, important modeling features suggested by prior studies from both the substantive and statistical areas, how the current model answers the research questions and what additional works need to be done, and effective and efficient presentation of the study findings.

1. Testing Interactive Effects

A statistical analysis often tests significant interactions. An interaction means that the impact of an independent variable on hazard rate varies by the level of another independent variable. Other terms used interchangeably with interaction include *buffering, moderating,* or *joint effects.* An interaction effect should be conceptually distinguished from a mediation effect (Baron & Kenny, 1986).

In a Cox regression, the analyst simply creates a product term of two independent variables and includes the product term, in addition to the two original variables, in the equation. Suppose analysts need to test the interaction of x_2 and x_3; they create a product term of the two variables (i.e., $x_4 = (x_2) \times (x_3)$), and include the original variables and the product term in the Cox regression, as

$$h_i(t) = h_0(t)\exp(\beta_1 x_{1i} + \beta_2 x_{2i} + \beta_3 x_{3i} + \beta_4 x_{4i})$$

By doing so, the analyst finds that the estimated coefficient $\hat{\beta}_2$ is the main effect of x_2, the estimated coefficient $\hat{\beta}_3$ is the main effect of x_2, and the estimated coefficient $\hat{\beta}_4$ is the interactive effect of x_2 and x_3.

Ideally, testing interactive effects should be guided by prior studies or research questions. However, if the study is new and few prior studies exist in the field, the analyst may use a data-driven approach to search all possible interactions and present the final model that includes only significant interactions.

Because an interactive effect involves three regression coefficients (i.e., the coefficients of the two main variables plus the coefficient of the product term), hazard ratios are not good for a meaningful presentation in the current context. The researcher may consider using a graph to present such an interactive effect. Figure 4.1 shows an example. The figure is a reprint of that presented by Wells and Guo (2004), in which the authors found that the mother's average monthly total income interacts with the entry cohort ($p<.05$). With such a figure, the interactive effect can be clearly interpreted as follows:

> In this figure, the speed of reunification was set at one for children from the postreform sample whose mothers had no income. The speed of reunification for all other children is compared with that group, controlling for other variables in the analysis besides the interaction term. Based on this convention, the figure highlights two comparisons: the effect of average monthly total postplacement income differs by sample, so that, for example, a one-dollar increase in a mother's income increases the speed with which her child returns home to a greater extent in the postreform sample than in the prereform sample; and there are large differences in speed of reunification for children whose mothers have the same relatively large income ($2,500) between samples. For example, children with mothers who had this income level in the prereform sample spent approximately 3.5 months in care (a speed of five), compared with 1 month in care (a speed of 17) for children in the postreform sample. (Wells & Guo, 2004, pp. 85–87)

The interaction figure was produced by using the three estimated regression coefficients. Denoting "entry cohort" as x_1 and its estimated coefficient as $\hat{\beta}_1$, "mother's income" as x_2 and its estimated coefficient as $\hat{\beta}_2$, the interaction as x_1x_2 and its estimated coefficient as $\hat{\beta}_3$, we basically extracted the three coefficients from the output (i.e., only these three coefficients) and omitted all other estimated coefficients not used for creation of the interaction figure. From the output, we found that $\hat{\beta}_1 = .3781573, \hat{\beta}_2 = .0011429$, and $\hat{\beta}_3 = -.000662$. Thus, the estimated hazard rate of reunification for a child who has zero values on all other variables (i.e., by constraining all other variables to be zero) is as follows:

$$\hat{h}(t) = \exp(.3781573x_1 + .0011429x_2 - .000662x_1x_2).$$

Using an Excel program, we set up the above equation and inserted different values for x_1 and x_2 into the equation to let the entry cohort be

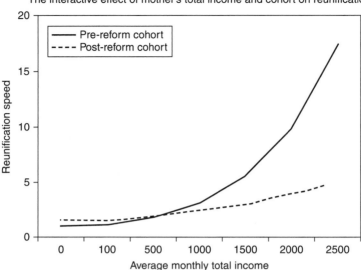

Figure 4.1 Example of presenting interactive effect based on estimated Cox regression.

the prereform cohort and postreform cohort, and to let income have values of $0, $100, $500, $1,000, $1,500, $2,000, and $2,500. The calculation was based on all possible combinations of values from these two variables. Thus, the above process produced a total of $2 \times 7 = 14$ values. Plotting these values by using the Excel's graphic program, we finally obtained the interaction graph shown as Figure 4.1.

2. Model-Predicted Survivor Curves

An efficient and effective presentation of study results estimated by a Cox regression may involve the use of model-predicted survivor curves. This curve is similar to those depicted in Chapter 2. The difference is that in Chapter 2, the survivor curves of different groups were estimated by the Kaplan-Meier method, a bivariate approach that does not control for all other covariates. With an estimated Cox regression, we now can present a similar survivor plot but control all other variables (i.e., variables are important to be controlled for but do not serve the purpose of investigating a particular effect the study centers on).

Most computing software packages offer graphic functions to produce model-based survivor curves and more. Allison (1995, pp. 165–173) describes how the BASELINE key word is used in SAS Proc Phreg to fulfill this task. Specifically, based on an estimated Cox model, the analyst can employ the following equation to obtain the model-predicted survivor curve:

$$S_i(t) = [S_0(t)]^{\exp(\beta_1\bar{x}_1 + \beta_2\bar{x}_2 + \beta_3\bar{x}_3 + \beta_4 x_4)}$$

where the Cox model includes four independent variables. The predicted curves specify the mean value of three variables (i.e., x_1, x_2, and x_3) and allow the variable of interest (i.e., x_4) to have different values.

Figures 4.2 and 4.3 show the model-predicted curves of a similar estimated Cox model presented in the illustrating example of the prior

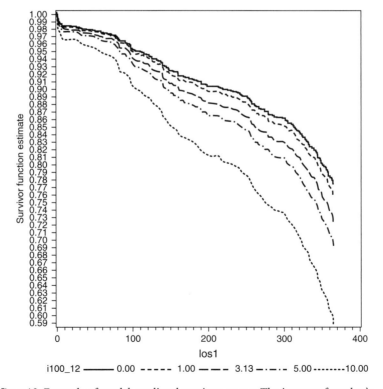

Figure 4.2 Example of model-predicted survivor curves: The impact of mother's average monthly total income from AFDC or TANF or wages on reunification.

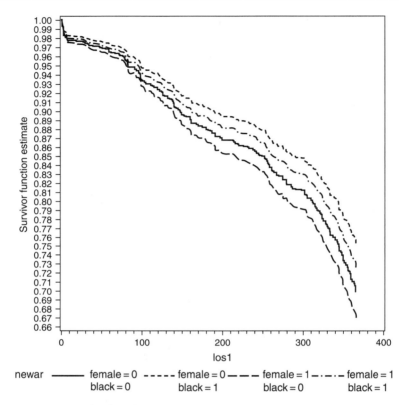

Figure 4.3 Example of model-predicted survivor curves: Racial and gender differences on reunification.

section.[1] Figure 4.2 shows the impact of income on reunification speed. To plot the model-predicted survivor curve, I used sample mean values for all variables used in the Cox regression (i.e., entry cohort, age, gender, etc.) but allowed mother's monthly total income from AFDC or TANF or wages to have five different values. Hence, the figure shows the survival experiences for five groups of children whose mothers have different incomes. In this figure, the bottom curve is the survival experience for children whose mothers' monthly income is $1,000, and the plot indicates that this group has the fastest speed in achieving reunification. The top curve is the survival experience for children whose mothers' monthly income is 0, and the plot indicates that this group has the slowest speed in achieving reunification. Figure 4.3

shows similar survivor curves for four groups who have different characteristics on gender and race.

3. Strategies for Using Time-Varying Covariates

Consider a hypothetical data set containing the following variables and observed values for one subject:

ID	LOS	Event	Age	Sex	Race	Program	B1	B2	B3	B4	B5	B6	B7	B8	...	B18
1	8	1	5.1	1	1	0	0	1	1	0	1	1	0	1	...	0

In this hypothetical data, *LOS* is length of time (in months) a study child stays in a mental health treatment program; *event* indicates event occurrence ($= 1$) or censored ($= 0$); *Age* is the age at entry measured in years; $Sex = 1$ if the study child is male and $Sex = 0$ if the study child is female; $Race = 1$ if the study child is African American and $Race = 0$ if the study child is of another race; $Program = 1$ if the study child is in a residential treatment program and $Program = 0$ if the study child is in other programs; and *B1* to *B18* are 18 dummy variables measuring disturbance behavior in each of the18-month study windows (e.g., $B1 = 1$ if the child's disturbance behavior is positive in the first month; and $B1 = 0$ if the child's disturbance behavior is not positive in the first month; the remainder of these variables are coded in the same way but measure disturbance behavior from months 2 to 18).

Thus, the 18 dummy variables may be used as a time-varying covariate in the study and linked to event times to examine the impact of disturbance behavior on length of stay in the program. With this kind of data, the analyst has at least five choices or models in which to use the time-varying information.

> Model 1: specify the disturbance behavior as a time-varying covariate and link the study time to the behavior variable in the current month;
>
> Model 2: specify the disturbance behavior as a time-varying covariate but use a 1 month lag, that is, link the study time to the behavior

variable 1 month earlier; the rationale of using a lagged variable is that it takes 1 month for the behavior variable to have an impact on the length of stay in the program;

Model 3: specify the disturbance behavior as a time-varying covariate but link the study time to the behavior variable for both the current month and 1 month earlier; this is a specification combining the previous two methods;

Model 4: specify the disturbance behavior as a time-fixed covariate but operate the variable as a number of cumulative positive months prior to exit or being censored; for the illustrated child, the analyst finds that by the time the child exited the program (i.e., in the eighth month), the child had a count of cumulative positive months of 5; specifically, based on variables *B1 to B18*, the analyst creates 18 variables *CPM1* to *CPM18* to count the number of cumulative positive months; the illustrated child's data on these new variables look like the following:

CPM1	CPM2	CPM3	CPM4	CPM5	CPM6	CPM7	CPM8	...	CPM18
0	1	2	2	3	4	4	5...	...	

Model 5: specify the disturbance behavior as a time-fixed covariate but operate the variable as a proportion of positive months prior to exit or being censored; for the illustrated child, the value on this variable is $(1+1+1+1+1)/8 = .625$; or 62.5% of the time during which the child stayed in the program, the child showed positive disturbance behavior.

Among the five, the first three models employ time-varying covariates, and each model links the disturbance behavior to the study time based on different conceptual considerations (i.e., is it the current behavior, or the 1 month lagged behavior, or behavior in both the current and the lagged months that affects the length of stay?). So the decision about choosing which model to use should be made on the basis of the researcher's conceptual model. Nonetheless, the two time-fixed models capture the same kinds of information and look into the relationship between behavior and length of stay also on a changing or moving basis. Therefore, the last two models, albeit time fixed, may not be a bad idea.

Table 4.4 Estimated Hazard Ratios of Five Models Using Different Strategies to Incorporate Time-Varying Covariates (Based on Hypothetical Data, n = 70)

Variable	Model 1	Model 2	Model 3	Model 4	Model 5
Age	1.11	1.1	1.08	1.05	1.07
Gender Male (Female is reference)	0.87	0.84	0.95	1.22	1.09
Race African American (Other is reference)	.45**	.46*	.40**	.52*	.48*
Program Residential (Other is reference)	.45**	.44**	.44**	.36**	.38**
Current Behavior	.04****		.08***		
Behavior 1 Month Lag		.08***	.15***		
Number of Cumulative Positive Months Prior to Exit				.61***	
Proportion of Positive Behavior Prior to Exit					.03***

*** $p<.001$, ** $p<.01$, * $p<.05$.

I created an artificial sample of 70 subjects on all the variables discussed above and ran all five Cox regressions using the artificial data. Results of these estimated models are shown in Table 4.4 and indicate that the last two models using time-fixed behavior measures work equally as well as the first three models.

The above example is based on artificial data, and the results may not be the same if we run these models in other data sets. However, the example sufficiently shows that time-varying information may be used differently; and as a consequence, the analyst does not have to use the time-varying information as time-varying covariates in a Cox regression. Indeed, researchers face many choices in modeling the longitudinal data and should examine their research questions and data in a careful manner, choosing a strategy that makes best sense, both conceptually and statistically.

4. Analysis of Competing Risks

In Chapter 3 I showed how to use a multinomial logit model to analyze competing risks. The same analysis can be implemented with the Cox regression. Basically, the analysis conducts separate Cox regressions, one at a time; each time the analyst codes one exit event as the event of interest and treats other types of exits as censoring. Taking the multiple-exits study illustrated in Chapter 3 as an example, to analyze competing risks of reunification and guardianship, the analyst needs to run two separate Cox models: the first model defines reunification as the event of interest and all other types of exits including guardianship and right-hand censoring as censoring; the second model defines guardianship as the event of interest and all other types of exits including reunification and right-hand censoring as censoring. After obtaining the estimated Cox models for both events, the analyst compares the significant coefficients between the two models to conduct a competing risks analysis; particularly, one examines whether the timing of having either event is associated with different determinants and probes why this is the case. For more information on conducting competing risks analysis with a Cox regression, readers are referred to Allison (1995, chapter 6).

5. Nonproportional Hazards Model

In some cases, researchers need to test whether the impact of an independent variable on the timing of event occurrence changes over time. That is, even though the independent variable is not time-varying, the researcher may create a time-varying covariate and test its interaction with the study time. The model can be easily established by including an interaction term (i.e., a product of an independent variable and the study time) in the equation. As depicted earlier, whenever the analyst introduces time-varying covariates into a Cox regression, the model is no longer proportional hazards because the impact of time-varying covariates changes at different rates for different individuals, and the ratios of their hazards cannot remain constant. Hence, models of this type are called nonproportional hazards models.

Formally, suppose t is study time, and x is a time-fixed variable; the analyst creates a product term xt and includes the term in the equation. Doing so, the model becomes

$$\log h(t) = \alpha(t) + \beta_1 x_1 + \beta_2 xt.$$

Factoring out the x, we obtain

$$\log h(t) = \alpha(t) + (\beta_1 + \beta_2 t)x.$$

The model shows that the effect of x on $log\ h(t)$ is $(\beta_1 + \beta_2 t)$. If β_2 is positive, then the effect of x increases linearly with time; if it is negative, the effect decreases linearly with time. By this setup, β_1 can be interpreted as the effect of x at time 0, the origin of the process (Allison, 1995).

The nonproportional hazards model is useful for testing theoretically derived hypotheses about influences of certain covariates, particularly about their time-varying nature. In program evaluation, researchers may use this model to test hypotheses about the time-varying impact of treatment, that is, to test whether the impact of treatment changes over time. For more information about nonproportional hazards model, readers are referred to Allison (1995, pp. 154–161).

6. Incorporating Sampling Weights into the Cox Regression

Many projects in social work research involve the use of national samples (e.g., the National Survey of Child and Adolescent Well-Being or NSCAW) that employ nonequal probabilities in sample selection for different study subjects. When conducting statistical analysis, researchers need to incorporate the sampling weights into the inferences so that the final findings are applicable to the original population the sample aims to represent. The Cox regression can be easily modified to incorporate sampling weights. Special software programs such as *SUDAAN* were designed to handle this type of data, known as *complex sampling*. Common software packages such as *Stata* can also be used, with appropriate specification of key words, to adjust sampling weights. These programs accomplish the goal by applying sampling weights to the partial likelihood function. Incorporating sampling weights, the partial likelihood equation (4.2) becomes

$$PL = \prod_{i=1}^{n} \left[\frac{e^{\beta x_i}}{\displaystyle\sum_{j=1}^{n} w_j Y_{ij} e^{\beta x_i}} \right]^{\delta_i w_i}$$

where w_i or w_j is the sampling weight for subject i or j (RTI, 2002).

7. Statistical Power Analysis

Ever since the seminal work of Cohen (1988), statistical power analysis has become a routine procedure of statistical analysis in the social behavioral sciences. It is often a required piece for grant applications and is also a crucial component of critical review of prior studies. A power analysis deals with four elements: the sample size N, the statistical significance or probability of making a type I error α, the statistical power or the ability to reject a false hypothesis (i.e., $1-\beta$, where β is the probability of making a type II error), and effect size. Different statistical analyses define effect size differently. In survival analysis, particularly in applications of the Cox regression, effect size refers to hazard ratio. Hence, if a study finds a hazard ratio of 2 between treated and control participants on having a certain event, the researcher may conclude that the hazard rate for treated participants is twice as fast as (or 100% faster than) the hazard rate for controls to have the event. Then the researcher wonders whether the study's finding about this effect size has adequate power, that is, whether the study can adequately reject a false hypothesis about no difference in the hazard rates between the two groups of participants. Typically, researchers fix the statistical significance at .05 and a statistical power at .80. In this context, two types of power analysis emerge: *(a)* at the planning stage of a new study, the researcher asks: to accomplish a statistical significance of .05, a statistical power of .80, and an effect size of 2, how many study participants (N) are needed? and *(b)* in a critical review study, the reviewer asks: given the sample size N, a statistical significance of .05, and the study's finding of effect size 2, does the study have an adequate power of .80? For applying statistical power analysis to social work research, readers are referred to Dattalo (2008), which is a comprehensive guide for determining sample size to maintain adequate statistical power for most analytical models.

The framework of power analysis for the Cox regression was developed by Schoenfeld (1983); the author basically focused on a binary or categorical covariate to define effect size. Hsieh and Lavori (2000) extended Schoenfeld's work to the case of continuous covariates. *Stata* offers two computing procedures for power analysis and determination of needed sample size: for power analysis in the context of the Cox regression, it offers a program called *stpower cox*; and for power analysis in a more general context of survival modeling (i.e., comparing two survivor functions using the log-rank test or the exponential test, as well as power analysis for the Cox regression), it offers a program called *stpower*. Users may also find free software packages computing power and sample size on the Internet. For instance, the program *PS* developed by Dupont and Plummer (2004) is such a free package. Power analysis for the Cox regression is just one of several functions provided by *PS*, and the software is user friendly. For a comprehensive overview of statistical power analysis for survival modeling and illustrations, readers are referred to Collett (1994, chapter 9).

5

The Parametric Models

P rior to the Cox regression, the parametric models were the leading
approaches to multivariate analysis of time-to-event data. The
advantages of parametric models include the following: *(a)* they allow
the user to run models including left-hand and interval censorings; and
(b) when assumptions about survival distribution are tenable, the estimates provided by the model are usually good, unbiased, and efficient.
The disadvantages of these models are these: *(a)* they cannot be used to
analyze time-varying covariates; and *(b)* they require prior knowledge
about the nature of the survival distribution being analyzed; if such
information is not available, the user must assume that the empirical
distribution being analyzed is the same distribution suggested by the
parametric model; and when such an assumption is not valid and the
actual distribution is not the same kind of distribution suggested by the
model, the user obtains misleading and biased results. Because of these
reasons, parametric models have been replaced by the Cox model in
practice.

In this book, I provide a brief review of the parametric models for
two reasons: *(a)* this is the method from which the contemporary
survival analysis originates; particularly, the model is an extension of
the traditional *ordinary least squares* (OLS) regression; understanding
the main features of parametric models helps users understand the
fundamental concepts of survival analysis as well as important statistical

concepts in general; and *(b)* the parametric models can be used to solve unique problems, such as handling left-hand and interval censorings; one of interesting parametric models is the piecewise exponential model, which is widely applied by social, health, and behavioral scientists.

This chapter follows Allison (1995, chapter 4). For more detailed information about the parametric models, readers are referred to Collett (1994), and Hosmer and Lemeshow (1999).

THE LINKAGE BETWEEN OLS REGRESSION AND THE PARAMETRIC MODELS

A natural starting point to learn parametric models is to consider the setup of an OLS regression. Let $Y = X \beta + e$ represent a population regression model, where Y is an $(n \times 1)$ vector of the dependent variable for the n participants, X is an $(n \times p)$ matrix containing a unit column (i.e., all elements in the column take value 1) and $p-1$ independent variables, e is an $(n \times 1)$ vector of the error term, and β is a $(p \times 1)$ vector of regression coefficients containing one intercept and $p-1$ slopes. Assuming repeated sampling and fixed X, and $e \sim iid$, $N(0, \sigma^2 I_n)$, where I_n is an $(n \times n)$ identity matrix and σ^2 is a scalar, so that $\sigma^2 I_n = E(ee')$ is the variance-covariance matrix of the error term. With the observed data of Y and X, we can use the least-squares criterion to choose the estimate of the coefficient vector β that makes the sum of the squared errors of the error vector e a minimum; that is, we minimize the quadratic form of the error vector. The least-squares estimator then provides an optimizing vector β, that is,

$$\beta = (X'X)^{-1}X'Y.$$

If we have sample data and use lower-case letters to represent sample variables and statistics, we have the sample estimated vector of regression coefficients as

$$b = (x'x)^{-1}x'y.$$

One of the crucial assumptions embedded in the OLS regression is that the dependent variable Y and the error term e in $Y = X \beta + e$ are subject to a normal distribution. If we relax this assumption by allowing Y and the error term e to follow other types of parametric distributions and use a maximum likelihood estimator instead of least-squares, then the model becomes a parametric model.

Parametric distributions are distributions whose mathematic properties (i.e., relationships among key statistics such as central tendency, quantiles, and dispersion) have been revealed by a few known functions and parameters. By this definition, a normal distribution is also a parametric distribution. However, in survival analysis, when researchers use the term, they typically refer to a non-normal parametric distribution. Evans, Hastings, and Peacock (2000) provide a good reference reviewing statistical distributions. The types of parametric distributions employed in survival analysis include exponential, Weibull, Gompertz, standard gamma, generalized gamma, lognormal, and log-logistic distributions. And the first three distributions fall into the same category of "exponential-family distributions" because by constraining certain parameters, Weibull and Gompertz distributions become exponential distributions. All these models take the form of an OLS regression, that is,

$$Y = X\beta + e = \beta_0 + \beta_1 X_1 + \ldots \beta_k X_k + e,$$

but assume a non-normal distribution for Y and e, except that the lognormal model still assumes a normal distribution. More explicitly, the dependent variable of a parametric model is $log\ T$, or the logarithm of study time (survival time) that follows a known parametric distribution; as such, the error term of the equation also follows a non-normal distribution.

Note that the dependent variable of a parametric model is $log\ T$. Since taking logarithms is a monotonic transformation, the study time and the log of study time should change in the same direction, such that the longer the study time, the higher the value of $log\ T$. Thus, the dependent variable is basically a measure of the length of time remaining in a state of nonoccurrence of the event of interest. With such a definition, the dependent variable is categorically different from that in the discrete-time model that defines probability as the dependent variable, and from that in the Cox regression that defines hazard rate as the dependent variable. The difference centers on the sign of an estimated regression coefficient. This is because a long study time (i.e., a high value on *log T*) is associated with a low probability of event occurrence [(i.e., a low value on *P(Y = 1)*)] or a low hazard rate [i.e., a low value on *h(t)*]. So comparing regression coefficients estimated from a parametric model, the analyst needs to reverse the sign of the regression coefficients (i.e., to make positive estimated coefficients negative, and negative coefficients positive), and then compare the reverse-signed coefficients with coefficients estimated by the discrete-time model or Cox regression. Only the reverse-signed coefficients are comparable to the coefficients of discrete-time and Cox models.

THE EXPONENTIAL MODEL

The primary feature of an exponential model is that the study time *T* has a constant hazard rate over the study window; that is, the rate of change of this distribution does not vary over time, or $h(t) = \lambda$ for $0 \leq t < \infty$, where λ is a constant. Graphically, the hazard rate of an exponential distribution can be shown by Figure 5.1, where two hazard rates *h(t) = 1*

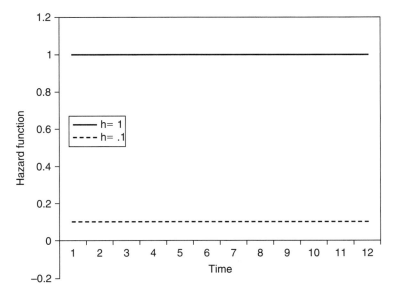

Figure 5.1 An illustration of the constant hazard rate assumed by the exponential model.

and $h(t) = .1$ are illustrated as a constant function of study time. As the figure shows, both hazard rates do not change values over time and become straight lines parallel to the time axis.

Statisticians have revealed key properties of an exponential distribution. Denoting λ as a constant hazard rate, the survivor function of the exponential distribution is $S(t) = e^{-\lambda t}$, the probability density function (PDF) of the distribution is $f(t) = \lambda e^{-\lambda t}$, the mean of the distribution is $\mu = \lambda^{-1}$, the median of the distribution is $t(50) = \frac{1}{\lambda} \log 2$, and the pth percentile of the distribution is $t(p) = \frac{1}{\lambda} \log \left(\frac{100}{100-p} \right)$.

If the study time T follows an exponential distribution, then the model regressing $\log T$ on covariates with $\sigma = 1$ is called an *exponential model*, or formally,

$$\log T_i = \beta_0 + \beta_1 x_{i1} + \dots + \beta_k x_{ik} + \sigma \varepsilon_i \tag{5.1}$$

where σ is constrained to be 1, ε has a standard extreme-value distribution, with constant mean and variance. The extreme-value distribution is unimodal and nonsymmetric, being slightly skewed to the left. The main purpose for taking the log transformation of T is to ensure that the predicted values of T are positive. σ is also known as a scale parameter. Later on I will introduce another parameter called a shape parameter.

If a researcher believes that the study time T is exponentially distributed, then he or she can run the model of (5.1) to estimate the impacts of predictors x_1 to x_k on $\log T$.

THE WEIBULL MODEL

The assumption about a constant hazard is rarely tenable in social, health, and behavioral applications. A more general distribution is the Weibull distribution that has a hazard function of

$$h(t) = \lambda \gamma t^{\gamma-1}, \text{ for } 0 < t < \infty.$$

This function depends on two parameters, λ and γ. When $\gamma = 1$, the hazard function is constant, that is, the survival times have an exponential distribution. So, an exponential distribution is a special case of a Weibull distribution.

Statisticians have revealed that the Weibull distribution has the following properties: the survivor function of the Weibull distribution is $S\{t\} = \exp(-\lambda t^{\gamma})$; the probability density function (PDF) of the distribution is $f(t) = \lambda \gamma t^{\gamma-1} \exp(-\lambda t^{\gamma})$; the mean of the distribution is $E(T) = \lambda^{-1/\gamma} \Gamma(\gamma^{-1} + 1)$, where $\Gamma(x)$ is a gamma function of

$$\Gamma(x) = \int_0^{\infty} u^{x-1} e^{-u} du;$$

the median of the distribution is $t(50) = \left\{ \frac{1}{\lambda} \log 2 \right\}^{1/\gamma}$; and the pth percentile of the distribution is $t(p) = \left\{ \frac{1}{\lambda} \log \left(\frac{100}{100-p} \right) \right\}^{1/\gamma}$.

The Weibull regression model has the same form as the exponential model (i.e., equation (5.1)):

$$\log T_i = \beta_0 + \beta_1 x_{i1} + \dots + \beta_k x_{ik} + \sigma \varepsilon_i$$

but relaxes the assumption of $\sigma = 1$. σ may be any positive value estimated on a basis of the sample data. When σ takes different values, the hazard rate h(t) is known to change in the following ways:

- When $\sigma = 1$, the distribution becomes exponential.
- When $\sigma > 1$, *h(t)* decreases with time.
- When .5 $< \sigma <$ 1, *h(t)* increases with time at a decreasing rate.
- When 0 $< \sigma <$ .5, *h(t)* increases with time at an increasing rate.
- When $\sigma = .5$, *h(t)* is a straight line with an origin at 0.

If a researcher believes that the study time T follows a Weibull distribution, then he or she can run the model of (5.1) to estimate the impacts of predictors x_1 to x_k on *log T*.

ASSESSING THE SUITABILITY OF APPLYING A PARAMETRIC MODEL

Other parametric models take a similar form to that of equation (5.1) but either make different assumptions about the known distribution or introduce additional parameters. For instance, the log-normal regression assumes a normal distribution of the error term ε instead of an extreme-value distribution. The generalized gamma model and standard gamma model introduce an additional parameter, called a *shape* parameter. For details of these models, readers may consult the references listed in the beginning of this chapter.

Because the analyst typically does not know what type of distribution is more appropriate to his or her data, the first task of running a parametric model is to assess the suitability of applying a parametric model. In this section, I describe three approaches to accomplishing this goal.

1. Examining the Hazard Function

This is a very preliminary and crude method for assessing suitability. Researchers run a univariate analysis to obtain estimates of hazard function $h(t)$ by using life-table or other approaches. Then they plot the hazard functions and examine the hazard plot to see how $h(t)$ changes over time. If $h(t)$ is approximately constant, an exponential model is appropriate; if $h(t)$ increases or decreases monotonically with the increase of study time T, then a Weibull model is appropriate.

2. Graphic Approaches

This is a widely applied approach to determine the suitability of applying certain parametric models. If the empirical data follow an exponential distribution, then a plot of $[-\log \hat{S}(t)]$ against study time t (known as a "log-survivor plot") should yield a straight line with an origin at time 0. If the empirical data follow a Weibull distribution, then a plot of $\log [-\log \hat{S}(t)]$ against *log t* (known as a "log-log survivor plot" or "log-cumulative-hazard plot") should yield a straight line. Figure 5.2 shows examples of these two plots based on the same data set. As the figure reveals, the curve shown by the "log-log survivor plot" appears to be a straighter line than that shown by the "log-survivor plot"; for this data set, a Weibull distribution is more plausible than an exponential distribution. To determine other types of models such as log-normal or log-logistic using graphic approaches, see Allison (1995, pp. 92–93). Graphics may also be obtained by running a parametric model first, and then the researcher examines the so-called residual plot (Allison, 1995, pp. 94–97).

3. Likelihood Ratio Test

The most formal way to assess the suitability of a parametric model is to perform a likelihood ratio test for nested models. The statistical definition

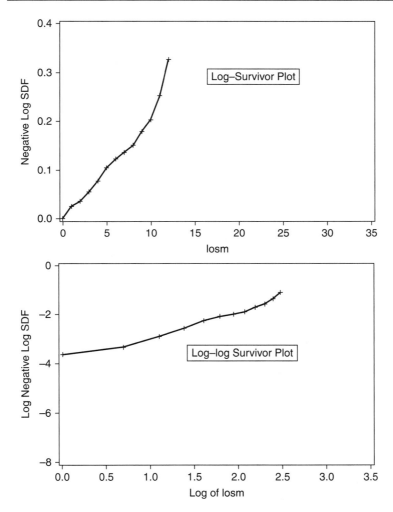

Figure 5.2 Log-survivor and log-log survivor plots based on hypothetical data.

of nested models is as follows: Model A is said to be nested within Model B if A is a special case of B; that is, A can be obtained by imposing restrictions on parameters in B. Thus, an exponential model is nested within a Weibull model because the scale parameter of the exponential model is constrained to be 1.

To evaluate whether model B is better than model A, the analyst calculates

$$-2[(log\ L\ for\ A) - (log\ L\ for\ B)],$$

where L stands for likelihood, and using df = number of constrained parameters to perform a chi-square test. If the p-value from the test is statistically significant (i.e., if $p<.05$), then the analyst concludes that model B is better than model A.

Using the same data introduced in Chapter 2 and illustrated in Chapter 3 with a discrete-time model and in Chapter 4 with a Cox regression, I ran several parametric models. I found that the log likelihood for the exponential model is -1027.64 and for the Weibull model is -1018.22. Between the two models, only one parameter (i.e., the scale parameter) is constrained, so $df = 1$. Performing the likelihood ratio test, I obtained $-2[(-1027.64)-(-1018.22)] = 18.84$. With df of 1, from a chi-square table I found that the p-value associated with this test is $<.0001$. Therefore, I concluded that the Weibull model is more suitable than the exponential model for my data set.

Using the same data set, I ran a few parametric models and conducted the likelihood ratio tests to determine which parametric models are suitable. Table 5.1 presents the results of these tests. The table indicates that the exponential model should be rejected; the generalized gamma model seems to be the best; and the Weibull model is also possible for this data set. Hence, I conclude that these two models should be retained as candidates of final models. Estimated regression coefficients, significance tests of study variables, and interpretation of these models will be presented in the final section of this chapter.

For a social work application of the parametric models, particularly application of the tests described above, readers are referred to Goerge (1990).

THE PIECEWISE EXPONENTIAL MODEL

Although in social behavioral sciences the exponential model is seldom applicable, a revised version of the exponential model, known as a *piecewise exponential model*, is very promising and may be applied to many empirical data sets to answer important research questions. For an

Table 5.1 Likelihood Ratio Tests Based on Nested Models

Contrast	Chi-square	df	p-value
Exponential vs. Weibull	18.84	1	0.000
Exponential vs. standard gamma	16.23	1	0.000
Exponential vs. g. gamma	22.95	2	0.000
Weibull vs g. gamma	4.11	1	0.043
Log-normal vs. g. gamma	9.07	1	0.003
Standard gamma vs. g. gamma	6.72	1	0.010

application example of the piecewise exponential model, readers are referred to Sandefur and Cook (1998), a study examining exit from receiving AFDC assistance.

The central idea of the piecewise model is this: while a constant hazard rate of a long study period ignores changes that occur in short time periods, a piecewise exponential assumption is flexible enough to do this and fits most applications. In other words, if the researcher can split the long study period into a series of short periods, it is probably reasonable to assume that within each short period the hazard rate is constant. Figure 5.3 illustrates this central idea assuming piecewise constant hazards.

Practically, the piecewise exponential model looks very similar to the discrete-time model that is based on a person-time data file. However, the piecewise exponent model has a more accurate measure of time than the discrete-time model. As such, the piecewise exponential model is usually applicable to many study settings.

There are two steps involved in running the piecewise exponential model. First, based on the person-level data, the analyst creates a person-time data file. The procedure is similar to that for creating the person-time data for the discrete-time model. That is, the analyst defines the study window (e.g., 12 months) and the metric of the time unit (e.g.,

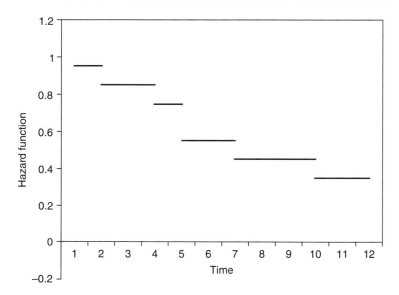

Figure 5.3 An illustration of the meaning of the piecewise exponential model.

bi-months). However, it differs from the procedure for creating the person-time data for a discrete-time model in the following ways: the analyst needs to create two dependent variables instead of one for the piecewise model (one is duration measuring the length of time for each data line, and the other is the censoring code indicating event occurrence or censoring). And second, after creating the person-time data, the analyst runs an exponential model based on the person-time data to obtain model estimates.

Table 5.2 illustrates the similarities and differences between the two types of person-time data files (i.e., one is for the piecewise exponential model, and the other is for the discrete-time model). For this illustration, I used a 12-month study window and a bi-month time metric, so a subject may contribute up to six data lines in the person-time data. The similarities between the two files include the following: (a) the number of data lines (i.e., person times) each subject contributes is exactly the same between the two files; (b) the total number of data lines is exactly the same between the two files—in this illustration, I had a total of 1,278 subjects; after conversion from the person data to person-time data, the

Table 5.2 Comparison of Data Structure Between the File for the Piecewise Exponential Model and the File for the Discrete-Time Model

	Obs	id	losp1	cen_r	los	bm	time	reunify
	1	1	129.00	1	3	1	2.00000	0
Data 1:	2	1	129.00	1	3	2	2.00000	0
Piecewise	3	1	129.00	1	3	3	0.23819	0
exponential	4	2	180.00	0	3	1	2.00000	0
	5	2	180.00	0	3	2	2.00000	0
	6	2	180.00	0	3	3	1.91376	1

	Obs	id	losp1	cen_r	bm	reunify	
	1	1	129.00	1	1	0	2 months each. These 2 lines represent 4 months (2x2=4) or 121.75 days.
Data 2:	2	1	129.00	1	2	0	
Discrete	3	1	129.00	1	3	0	
- time	4	2	180.00	0	1	0	1.91376 x 30.4375 = 58.25 days
	5	2	180.00	0	2	0	
	6	2	180.00	0	3	1	That is, 180-121.75 = 58.25

Obs: observed data line.
id: identification number.
losp1: length of stay in the first spell of foster care (days).
cen_r: censoring code (1 censored, 0 event reunification).
los: length of time measured in bi-month.
bm: bi-month indicator.
time: length of time variable created for the piecewise exponential model.
reunify: a binary event code indicate event occurrence.

total number of data lines is 6,112 for both files; and (c) the event code (i.e., named *reunify*) is exactly the same between the two files.

The differences between the two files are these. First, the discrete-time file does not contain a *time* variable measuring study time, but the piecewise exponential file does; and the piecewise exponential file has a precise measure of time for each data line or person-bi-months. The second difference is worth explanation. Note how the piecewise exponential file converts the length of time from the person data to the person-time data: for subject *id* = 2, the study time *losp1* = 180 days is shown by the person file, so this subject's time equals 180/30.4375 = 5.91375 months. Because each data line represents 2 months, the subject then contributes three data lines; the first two lines have a value of 2.0000 on the *time* variable, and the third data line on *time* is simply the remaining time from *losp1* (i.e., $180 - 4(30.4375) = 58.25$ days, and 58.25 days is equal to 1.91376 months = 58.25/30.4375); thus, the third data line for this subject is coded 1.91376 on *time*.

With this data set, we can run the exponential parametric model. In running the model, the hazard rates vary by person-time, not by person; and therefore, the hazard rate is constant within each person-time or each bi-month for this example. As the data file shows, the length of time unit affects the estimation: if the analyst believes that the hazard rate changes in a period shorter than 2 months, then a refined time metric such as 1 month may be used.

AN ILLUSTRATING EXAMPLE AND MODEL COMPARISONS

To illustrate the estimation and interpretation of parametric models, I ran two parametric models (i.e., the Weibull and the generalized gamma models, because the likelihood ratio tests indicate that only these two parametric models are suitable), and two piecewise exponential models (i.e., one with time-varying covariates and one with time-fixed covariates) on the same data used in the reunification study. For model comparisons, I added results of the discrete-time model and the Cox regression to the final table (see Table 5.3). The main findings of the table are summarized below.

First, to make the results of the parametric models comparable to those of the discrete-time and Cox models, I reversed the sign for all regression coefficients estimated by the parametric models. That is, the columns for these models are labeled "$-B$," and the columns for the discrete-time and Cox models are labeled "B."

Second is the problem of how to interpret regression coefficients estimated by a parametric model. Let's focus on coefficients for the dummy variables first. Suppose we want to interpret the coefficient of "age 0" estimated by the Weibull model. $-B$ for this variable is $-.478$. Reversing it back to its original value (because for now I focus on the interpretation of coefficients, not on model comparisons), B for "age 0" = .478. Remember that a parametric model uses $log\ T$ as the dependent variable, so we need to take the exponent of B to ease the interpretation; doing so, we obtain $e^B = e^{.478} = 1.613$. Therefore, controlling for all other

Table 5.3 Model Comparisons

Variable	Weibull -B	Generalized Gamma -B	Piecewise Exponential (1) -B	Piecewise Exponential (2) -B	Discrete-Time B	Cox Regression B
Entry cohort (prereform)						
Postreform 1	.071	−.019	−.048	.037	−.077	−.045
Postreform 2	−.031	−.096	−.195	−.116	−.244	−.193
Child age at entry (8–11)						
0	−.478 ⋆	−.546 ⋆	−.418 ⋆	−.384 ⋆	−.419 ⋆	−.415 ⋆
1–3	−.059	−.144	−.137	−.066	−.147	−.132
4–7	−.290	−.367	−.274	−.221	−.287	−.276
12–16	−.189	−.292	−.136	−.119	−.167	−.133
Child gender (male)						
Female	.114	.145	.101	.121	.099	.098
Child race (other)						
African American	−.290	−.363 ⋆	−.224	−.234	−.214	−.222
Reason for placement (physical abuse)						
Neglect	−.800 ⋆⋆	−.850 ⋆⋆	−.704 ⋆⋆	−.589 ⋆⋆	−.725 ⋆⋆	−.709 ⋆⋆
Dependency	−.489	−.560	−.445 ⋆	−.333	−.463 ⋆	−.447 ⋆
Other	−.903 ⋆⋆	−.919 ⋆⋆	−.719 ⋆⋆	−.645 ⋆⋆	−.733⋆⋆	−.720 ⋆⋆
First placement type (kinship)						
Foster	.139	.207	.126	.156	.173	.118
Other	−.267	−.262	−.214	−.179	−.197	−.221

continued

Table 5.3 (Continued)

Variable	Weibull -B	Generalized Gamma -B	Piecewise Expnential (1) -B	Piecewise Exponential (2) -B	Discrete-Time B	Cox Regression B
Mother's income from TANF & wages (2-month lag, time varying, in $100)					.042**	.040**
Mother's income from TANF & wages (Total monthly average prior to exit)	.001**	.001**	.040**	.001**		
% mother's income due to wages (2-month lag, time varying, 10% points)			-.022		-.001	-.022
% mother's income due to wages (Prior to exit)	-.007**	-.009**		-.006**		
Scale	1.242	1.605	1.000	1.000		
Shape		.599				
P-value for the Larange multiplier test			p=.1423	p=.1557		
Number of study subjects	1,278	1,278	1,278	1,278	1,278	
Number of subject-bi-months			6,112	6,112	6,112	

*p < .05, **p < .01.
Note: A highlighted entry is an estimate whose sign and/or significance level are(is) different from its corresponding entry estimated by the Cox regression.

variables, the expected time to stay in foster care before reunification for children "aged 0 at entry" is 61.3% longer than for children "aged 8–11 at entry." The interpretation of regression coefficients for other coefficients of dummy variables from all parametric models can be performed in this fashion. Let's take the coefficient for a continuous variable (say, "% of mother's income due to wages") as a second example. The Weibull model shows that $-B$ of "% of mother's income due to wages" is $-.007$. Reversing the sign, we obtain $B = .007$. For a continuous variable, we can use the transformation $100(e^B - 1)$, which gives the percentage increase in the expected study time for each one-unit increase in the variable. Thus, $100(e^B - 1) = 100(e^{.007} - 1) = 100(1.007 - 1) = 0.702$, meaning that controlling for all other variables, each 10 percentage point increase in mother's income due to wages is associated with a 0.7% increase in the child's expected time to stay in foster care before reunification. All other coefficients of continuous variables estimated by the parametric models can be interpreted in this fashion.

Third, although a parametric model cannot handle time-varying covariates, this is not the case for the piecewise exponential model. Just like a discrete-time model, a piecewise exponential model can sufficiently analyze time-varying covariates. This is because the piecewise model analyzes survival time using person-time data rather than person data. This is truly a unique advantage offered by the piecewise exponential model! The piecewise exponential model (1) of Table 5.3 shows $B = -.040$ for "mother's income from TANF and wages" on a time-varying basis with a 2-month lag. Thus, $100(e^B - 1) = 100(e^{-.04} - 1) = 100(.9608 - 1) = -3.92$, meaning that controlling for all other variables, each $100 increase in mother's total monthly average income 2 months earlier is associated with a 3.92% decrease in the child's expected time to stay in foster care before reunification ($p<.01$). Once again, the model confirms the importance of providing cash assistance to alleviate economic hardship for the biological mothers of foster children.

Finally, from a modeling perspective, we can compare all models for each variable. This is an important task for a rigorous statistical analysis. The reason for doing this is obvious: each statistical model has its own assumptions about the data set, and the analyst does not know the extent to which his data violate the assumptions. Although through a careful modeling process the analyst has checked the tenability of the assumptions, it is likely that important assumptions are violated and that estimates from the model are biased. Thus, for an important study like the current one, it is crucial to analyze the same data using different approaches and draw conclusions based on consistent findings from multiple models. It is for this reason (i.e., to permit model comparisons) that I reversed the sign of all coefficients estimated by the parametric models. To compare coefficients across models, I choose the Cox regression as a baseline model. Note that I chose the Cox regression not because it is the best model among all—we don't know whether this is case for the current study. I chose the Cox regression as a baseline purely arbitrarily, and any one of the six models can serve as a baseline model. To compare coefficients across models, I focus on two aspects: the sign of an estimated coefficient and whether the coefficient is statistically significant. Note that due to the nature of the dependent variable used by different models, the magnitude of a coefficient is not meaningful and comparable across models. Using the Cox regression as a baseline, I then checked each coefficient across the six models and highlighted the coefficient whose sign is contradictory to that of the Cox regression or whose significance pattern is different from that of the Cox regression. The results indicate three models showing exactly the same pattern, that is, the piecewise exponential model (1), the discrete-time model, and the Cox regression. This merely confirms our earlier knowledge about the robustness of these three models. The differences on "post-reform cohort 1" among these models can be ignored because none of the six models shows a significant coefficient for this variable. There is only one model (i.e., the generalized gamma model) that shows a significant coefficient for the variable "African American." Since the other five models do not show significance for this variable, we probably can conclude that this variable is not statistically significant. Therefore, the model comparison narrows down to only one variable that has contradictory patterns among models: the variable of "% of mother's income due to wages." A further investigation reveals that all significant coefficients on this variable used a time-fixed method, so the difference is really between time-varying and time-fixed methods. Thus, the model comparisons lead us to choose any one of three models (i.e., Cox regression, or discrete-time model, or piecewise exponential (1)) as our final model, and based on one of the three sets of coefficients, we can interpret and present our final findings. With an uncertain finding about whether "% of mother's income due to wages" is statistically significant, we should clearly report it, treat the current investigation about this variable as inconclusive, and call for future studies of it.

Before concluding the chapter, I would like to offer a general comment about model comparison. As the illustrating example shows, it is important to conduct model comparisons, which offer numerous advantages. Among other things, comparison provides an effective and efficient tool for the researcher to test the sensitivity of study data to model assumptions, to check the robustness of a given analytic model, and most of all, to gain confidence about the study findings. In this example, I showed three approaches to choosing a "best" model: graphic, likelihood ratio test, and a comparison of substantive findings about coefficient signs and significances.

6

Multilevel Analysis of Time-to-Event Data

This chapter focuses on a relatively new class of survival models: the multilevel approaches to time-to-event data. In this chapter, I first review the importance of conducting multilevel analysis in social work research and the recent advances in biostatistics to correct for autocorrelated survival times. Next, I describe the independent assumption embedded in the Cox proportional hazards model and detail the negative consequence of inclusion of autocorrelated data. I then review available biomedical research models that correct for autocorrelation, particularly, the WLW method. Finally, using empirical data, I illustrate how to diagnose the presence of autocorrelation and how to use one such corrective model. Most of the content presented in this chapter is based on Guo and Wells (2003).

GROUPED DATA AND SIGNIFICANCE OF CONDUCTING MULTILEVEL ANALYSIS

Social work researchers often encounter grouped or multilevel data in which individuals are nested within families, and families are nested within neighborhoods. Analyzing such data requires special treatment because most multivariate models assume that observations are independent, and grouped data clearly violate this assumption.

Sibling-group data are such an example of violating the independent assumption. These types of data often include children from the same family who exit or reenter foster care at roughly the same time. Placement of siblings in the same home is mandated by many states or is the preference of many public agencies (Hegar, 1988; Smith, 1996).

A more important reason for conducting multilevel modeling is substantive: researchers need to test how individual characteristics interact with family characteristics, or how clients' characteristics interact with agency characteristics, and therefore, to test joint effects of the two-level characteristics on the outcome variable. For instance, in child welfare research, an important research question is this: what is the joint impact of a child's receipt of welfare and his or her mother's receipt of welfare on foster care outcomes? How are agency performance outcomes related to local county and agency factors as well as individual factors of the child? This type of cross-level interaction, or propositions about macro-to-micro relations, cannot be answered by investigations using conventional approaches.

Statisticians and biomedical researchers identified adverse consequences of applying the Cox regression to grouped survival times (Andersen & Gill, 1982; Prentice, Williams, & Peterson, 1981). They noted that when the independent assumption of the Cox model is violated, the tests of statistical significance are biased and in ways that cannot be predicted beforehand (Wei, Lin, & Weissfeld, 1989). Significant progress has been made toward a solution to the problem of nonindependent event times. Several approaches have been applied in biomedical research (Andersen & Gill, 1982; Lee, Wei, & Amato, 1992; Liang, Self, & Chang, 1993; Prentice et al., 1981; Wei et al., 1989).

CONSEQUENCES OF USING AUTOCORRELATED DATA

To detail the consequences of including autocorrelated data in the Cox proportional hazards model, it is useful to clarify a primary assumption underlying the method. The Cox regression, like all regression-type models, assumes that use of the model with data from the same unit (such as a person, a sibling group, a family, or an organization) violates the assumption about independent event data. This is because data from the same unit tend to be more alike than data from independent units (Allison, 1995). Use of the Cox model without appropriately applying a procedure to correct for autocorrelated data causes the estimation procedure to assume the sample contains more information than it actually has (Allison, 1995, p. 240).

The major consequence of including autocorrelated data in the Cox proportional hazards model is that the tests of statistical significance may be misleading. Studies using both real data and Monte Carlo experiments show that the standard errors produced by the Cox proportional hazards model are biased downward and that test statistics produced by the model are biased upward (Allison, 1995; Lin, 1994; Wei et al., 1989). As a result, the Cox model may identify some independent variables as statistically significant that are, in fact, statistically insignificant.

Grouped data may also lead to informative censoring. For instance, when a foster care study uses a sample that contains a high proportion of children who are siblings, the noninformative censoring assumption is very likely to be violated. This is because children from the same sibling group tend to have same length of time in foster care and a common outcome. Therefore, if one child in a sibling group is randomly censored, his or her siblings will also be randomly censored.

DIAGNOSTIC PROCEDURES

In spite of these consequences, no definitive tests have been developed to assess the severity of autocorrelation in a given study. Following the work of Allison (1995, chapter 8), I summarize below three procedures that may be used to diagnose the severity of autocorrelation in a given study. In the following exposition, I take data with sibling groups as an illustrating example.

1. Assess the Scope of the Problem

The first strategy is to examine study data to evaluate whether the presence of sibling-group data is a problem. Examination involves identification of the proportion of children with siblings in the sample. If the proportion is small, for example, 10% or less, the issue of autocorrelated data can be ignored. If the proportion is not small, for example, more than 10%, the researcher needs to examine the beginning and ending dates for the event under study. These may be the date on which a child leaves foster care and returns home. If the dates differ for siblings, the issue of autocorrelated data can be ignored. If the dates are frequently approximately the same, one needs to calculate the standard deviation of the length of time in care (or at home) within each sibling group. If the within-group standard deviations are small, on average, the sample's intragroup correlation is likely to be high, and a corrective procedure should be used in the analysis.

2. Assess the Intragroup Correlation

The second strategy is to assess directly the intra-sibling-group correlation by running hierarchical linear modeling, or HLM. (Before running the analysis, one needs to change the values of event times for censored subjects for whom the event under study occurred after the end of the study window to the length of the study window.)[1] The intragroup correlation is defined as the proportion of the variance in the transformed event times that is between groups (Raudenbush & Bryk, 2002). The intragroup correlation can be calculated by dividing the between-group variance by the sum of the between-group variance and the within-group variance. One can obtain the between-group and within-group variances by running a one-way ANOVA with random effects model in HLM. A high intragroup correlation, a correlation greater than .5, for example, is an indication that a considerable proportion of the variation in timing of an event is due to groups and that a corrected Cox model should be used in the analysis.

3. Assess the Effect of an Omitted Sibling's Length of Time in Care

The third strategy is to use the event time of a sibling omitted from each sibling group as one of the predictors in the Cox model. The model should also include any covariates one would otherwise include in the model because the question is whether there is *residual* autocorrelation after the effects of the covariates have been removed. This analysis is performed on a subset of the sample, that is, on only those who have a sibling in the sample. A significant coefficient for the event time of omitted siblings would indicate a high degree of intragroup correlation among the sibling groups, and a corrected model should be used in the analysis.

OVERVIEW OF THE MULTILEVEL APPROACHES

A variety of models have been developed to correct for the problems associated with autocorrelation. Terry M. Therneau and Patricia M. Grambsch (2000) and Philip Hougaard (2000) provide comprehensive evaluations of recent developments, the types of data for which each is best suited, and the computer software that is available for each one.

There are two types of autocorrelated multivariate event times. These are clustered event data, or correlated event times among subjects from the same group, and repeated event data, or the times the same event occurs more than once to the same subject.

Models to correct for autocorrelation induced by clustered event data fall into two broad categories: the frailty models and the marginal models. The frailty models include random effects to represent extra heterogeneity of the unit that gives rise to the dependence of event times (Clayton & Cuzick, 1985; Guo & Rodriguez, 1992; Hougaard, 1986, 1987; Klein, 1992; Nielsen, Gill, Andersen, & Sorensen, 1992; Oakes, 1989, 1992). In order to use frailty models, one must specify correctly a parametric distribution of the frailty (Lin, 1994), which is often unknown to researchers. The frailty models are best suited to clinical trials involving random selection of subjects or to samples involving matched-pairs covariates (Hougaard, 2000). In this text, I focus on marginal models because frailty models require stronger and more restrictive assumptions.

The following two models are developed to handle repeated events data: (a) the AG multiplicative intensity model (Andersen & Gill, 1982); under the specification of this model, the risk of a recurrent event for a subject satisfies the usual proportional hazards model and is unaffected by earlier events that occurred to the subjects unless terms that capture such dependence are included explicitly in the model as covariates (Lin, 1994); (b) the PWP Model (Prentice et al., 1981)—this model differs from the AG model in two aspects: the risk sets for the $(k+1)$th recurrences are restricted to the individuals who have experienced the first k recurrences, and the underlying intensity functions and regression parameters are allowed to vary among distinct recurrences (Wei et al., 1989).

Several computer software programs are available for fitting both frailty and marginal models. The statistical software package *S-Plus* offers an array of functions for fitting both frailty and marginal models. Several *SAS* macros, along with most of the data sets discussed in Therneau and Grambsch (2000), can be found in the companion Web page of their book. Several *SAS* macros developed by Allison can be downloaded from the *SAS* Web page. The *SAS Proc Phreg* and *Stata stcox* procedures offer the estimation of marginal approaches.

THE MARGINAL MODELS

The marginal models have much in common with the generalized estimating equation (GEE) approach of Zeger, Liang, and Albert (1988). Two marginal models are especially useful to the multilevel analysis of survival data: the WLW model (Wei et al., 1989), and the LWA model (Lee et al., 1992). These models are designated by the first initials of their developers' last names.[2]

The marginal models offer several advantages for multilevel analysis. They are flexible in that they do not require assumptions about the nature or structure of the dependence in correlated event times (Allison, 1995; Wei et al., 1989). They are applicable to moderate-sized samples (Wei et al., 1989).[3] They are consistent with the conventional Cox regression in the sense that the conventional model is a special case of the marginal models (Hougaard, 2000). The computation of a marginal model is relatively simple once a data set has been created (Therneau & Grambsch, 2000).

In general, both the WLW and the LWA models make no more assumptions about the data than does the conventional Cox regression. The fundamental difference between the WLW and LWA models is the way each handles the baseline hazard function (i.e., $h_0(t)$ in equation (4.1)). The WLW model allows the baseline hazard function to vary among types of multivariate event times and to consider type-specific regression parameters. By way of contrast, the LWA model postulates a common baseline hazard function for all types of event times (Lin, 1994).

Both models can be employed to facilitate multilevel analysis. The WLW model can be used whether subjects within groups have common or divergent baseline hazard rates whereas the LWA model can be used only when they have common baseline hazard rates. I now use the WLW model as one example to illustrate the methodology of correcting auto-correlated event times.

To correct for biases in standard errors and to estimate parameters, the WLW procedure runs a series of Cox regression models. To run these models, the subjects within groups must be organized randomly. The procedure requires that the investigator identify the subjects to be analyzed in the first and succeeding models. Taking the sibling group data as an example, the first model is for the first child selected from all sibling groups, the second is for the second child from all groups, and so on. The estimating procedure continues in this fashion until the number of children gets too small to estimate a model reliably. Based on the estimated variances, the WLW procedure then estimates the marginal distributions of the distinct event times in order to yield a robust and optimal estimation of the variance-covariance matrix. This variance-covariance matrix is then used in statistical testing. Standard errors from this matrix are usually larger than those estimated by the uncorrected model. Therefore, when autocorrelation is present, variables that are significant in the uncorrected Cox model may become insignificant in the Cox model corrected with the WLW procedure.[4]

Since the WLW model is designed to correct for biases in standard errors, the estimated coefficients from this procedure are not expected to differ in size from those produced by the uncorrected Cox model when both models are constructed with data from the same subjects (Allison, 1995). (If the estimated coefficients do differ, they can generally be ignored.) One limitation of the WLW procedure is that some subjects in groups will be excluded from the analysis when the distribution of group size is skewed.

To understand this limitation, suppose we analyze a sample of 40 children in three types of groups: (1) 10 groups of size one (i.e., single child without siblings), (2) 10 groups of size two (i.e., each group comprises two children coming from the same family), and (3) one group of size 10 (i.e., all 10 children coming from one family). The

WLW procedure will analyze all children from groups whose size is either one or two but only two children from the group of size 10. This is because when the WLW runs the third model for the third child from each sibling group, there is only one child left, that is, the third child from the group of size 10. The program WLW macro will stop at this point because the sample size becomes too small to reliably run a model. In this example, the WLW has to delete eight children or 20% of the sample from the study.

AN ILLUSTRATING EXAMPLE

In this illustration, we demonstrate how to use the diagnostic procedures described above. We also show the deficiencies of results from an uncorrected Cox model and results from a Cox model corrected by including a randomly selected child from each sibling group. We use data from an investigation designed to identify which of 12 factors are linked most strongly to timing of reunification of foster children within 18 months of entry into care (Wells & Guo, 2003). The study sample includes 525 children first placed in foster care over a 6-month period in the late 1990s.

1. Diagnosis of an Autocorrelation Problem

To illustrate how to diagnose the presence of autocorrelation in study data, we constructed a data set in which 58% of study children (n = 302) form 151 sibling groups each containing two siblings. The remaining children (n = 223) do not have a sibling in the sample. As a result, the distribution of the sibling group size, in this illustration, is not skewed. Our examination of the dates of entry into foster care and exit from foster care for subjects shows that children from the same sibling group often have the same dates of entry and exit. As a result, the length of time siblings spend in foster care is often the same. Of the 151 sibling groups, 116 or 76.8% have a standard deviation of zero for time spent in foster care prior to exit.

Then, we examined the degree of correlation among siblings' event data. We changed the lengths of stay for children who were censored at the end of the 18-month study window to 18 months, and then we used these transformed data to run a one-way ANOVA with random effects model in HLM. The between-group variance of length of stay is 33059.49, and the within group variance of length of stay is 5159.63. Together they yield an estimated intragroup correlation of 0.865. Therefore, the intragroup correlation in this data set is high: about 86.5% of the variation in length of stay in this sample is due to groups, and only 13.5% is due to individuals.

We also used the event time of a sibling who was omitted from the analysis as one of the predictors of timing of reunification. Following Allison's suggestion (1995), we ran an uncorrected Cox model using 151 children in the sample. The other predictor variables used in the model include child age at entry, gender, ethnicity, health status at entry, reason for a child's placement, the type of placement, mother's metal health status, mother's problem with substance abuse, and other mother's welfare use and employment variables. The coefficient "Duration of an omitted sibling" is -0.012 ($p<.0001$), and the hazard ratio is $\exp(-0.012) = 0.988$. This means that the omitted sibling's length of stay is highly predictive of the length of stay of the child in the omitted sibling's sibling group. The correlation is almost one: the hazard of reunification for any child included in the analysis is almost the same as the hazard of his or her omitted sibling, other things being equal.

As a result of these diagnostic procedures, one can conclude that the event data from sibling groups are highly correlated, that the assumption of the Cox proportional hazards model is violated, and that a correction for the biases introduced by these violations is necessary to have an efficient and a valid test of the statistical significance of each factor included in the model.

2. Demonstration of the Utility of the WLW Model

To demonstrate the utility of the WLW model, we conducted two comparative analyses. In the first analysis, we compared the results of the corrected Cox model (the WLW model) with those of the uncorrected Cox model ("Naïve" model 1). In the second comparison, we compared the results of the corrected Cox model (the WLW model) with those of a second naïve model, the random selection of one subject from a group to include in the analysis (Naïve model 2).

We used the SAS WLW macro written by Allison (1995, pp. 242–243) to estimate the WLW model. This macro can be run on SAS release 6.10 or higher and requires use of the Proc IML module. We used the SAS Proc Phreg to estimate both of the naïve models.

The WLW Model and the Naïve Model 1. In the first comparison, both analyses use the same 525 subjects. As the results in Table 6.1 show, most standard errors estimated by the Naïve model 1 are lower than the corresponding errors estimated by the WLW Model. As a result, the *p*-values in the WLW model have also changed. Naïve model 1 identifies one variable, "Received TANF income and lost TANF income," as statistically significant at the .001 level, and two variables, "Foster home" and "Percent time mother received TANF-pre-placement window," as statistically significant at the .05 level. Each of these variables is statistically insignificant at the same level in the WLW model. On the other hand, Naïve model 1 identifies the variable "Group home or hospital" as statistically insignificant, and the WLW model identifies the variable as statistically significant at the .001 level.

Table 6.1 also shows that at an alpha level of .05, the naïve model identifies 8 of 19 variables as statistically significant, but the WLW Model identifies as statistically significant 6 of those 8 variables, plus one variable that is statistically insignificant in the Naïve model 1.

The WLW Model and the Naïve Model 2. In the second analysis, we compared the results from the WLW model with those from the second uncorrected Cox model (the Naïve model 2). These models use different numbers of subjects: for the corrected model, 525 subjects, and for the uncorrected model, 374 subjects, as a result of the inclusion of only one randomly selected child from each sibling group.

As data in Table 6.1 show, the Naïve model 2 identifies as statistically insignificant one variable, "Group home or hospital," that is statistically significant at the .001 level in the WLW model. The Naïve model 2 identifies two variables as statistically insignificant, "Age 0" and "Mother mental problems: Presence," that are statistically significant at the .05 level in the WLW model. Table 6.1 also shows that the hazard ratios in the two models differ by 5 percentage points or more on the following eight variables: "Age 1–3," "Age 12–16," "Female," "Health problems at entry: Presence," "Dependency," "Reason for placement: Other," "Group home or hospital," and "Mother's substance abuse: Presence."

Table 6.1 Model Comparisons

Variable	Naïve Model 1: Same Set of Subjects as the WLW Model (n=525)				Naïve Model 2: Randomly Selected One Child from Each Sibling Group (n=374)				Robust Model WLW (n=525)			
	B	SE	p-value	Hazard Ratio	B	SE	p-value	Hazard Ratio	B	SE	p-value	Hazard Ratio
Age at entry (in years)												
8–11												
0	-0.6158*	0.3086	0.0460	0.540	-0.7072	0.3751	0.0593	0.493	-0.7397*	0.3742	0.0481	0.477
1–3	-0.0367	0.2795	0.8954	0.964	-0.1687	0.3623	0.6415	0.845	-0.0694	0.3282	0.8326	0.933
4–7	-0.1106	0.2785	0.6913	0.895	-0.1444	0.3702	0.6964	0.866	-0.1792	0.3071	0.5596	0.836
12–16	-0.1679	0.2683	0.5316	0.845	-0.3466	0.3519	0.3246	0.707	-0.1082	0.3157	0.7317	0.897
Gender												
Male												
Female	-0.0749	0.1769	0.6719	0.928	-0.4243	0.2188	0.0525	0.654	-0.1491	0.1876	0.4268	0.861
Ethnicity												
Non-African-American												
African American	-0.3379	0.1978	0.0876	0.713	-0.2420	0.2410	0.3153	0.785	-0.2564	0.2409	0.2871	0.774
Health problems at entry												
Absence												
Presence	-0.1808	0.1960	0.3563	0.835	-0.1225	0.2365	0.6044	0.885	-0.1854	0.2322	0.4247	0.831
Reason for placement												
Physical abuse												
Neglect	-0.9016***	0.2363	0.0001	0.406	-0.9684***	0.2936	0.0010	0.380	-0.9381***	0.2810	0.0008	0.391
Dependency	-0.1544	0.3142	0.6231	0.857	-0.2706	0.3846	0.4818	0.763	-0.1408	0.3875	0.7163	0.869
Other	-0.8223	0.6211	0.1855	0.439	-1.2673	0.7651	0.0976	0.282	-0.6175	0.5411	0.2538	0.539

First placement type

	Coeff.	SE	p	OR	Coeff.	SE	p	OR	Coeff.	SE	p	OR
Kinship home												
Foster home	-0.3950*	0.1890	0.0366	0.674	-0.4037	0.2351	0.0860	0.668	-0.3683	0.2314	0.1114	0.692
Group home or hospital	-0.9863	0.5459	0.0708	0.373	-0.8697	0.5622	0.1219	0.419	-2.7807***	0.5221	<0.0001	0.062
Mother mental problems												
Absence												
Presence	-0.7931*	0.3127	0.0112	0.452	-0.7437	0.4001	0.0631	0.475	-0.7403*	0.3695	0.0451	0.477
Mother substance abuse												
Absence												
Presence	-0.3593	0.1984	0.0702	0.698	-0.1851	0.2444	0.4488	0.831	-0.2942	0.2396	0.2194	0.745
Percent time mother received TANF - pre-placement window	0.0061*	0.0030	0.0445	1.006	0.0059	0.0039	0.1279	1.006	0.0061	0.0038	0.1089	1.006
Mother's receipt/loss TANF/ wages - post-placement window												
Received TANF, no loss												
Never received TANF income	0.3008	0.2801	0.2828	1.351	0.2185	0.3444	0.5258	1.244	0.2375	0.3306	0.4725	1.268
Received TANF income, and lost TANF income	-1.1978***	0.3223	0.0002	0.302	-1.1289**	0.3960	0.0044	0.323	-1.1700**	0.3809	0.0021	0.310
Mother's average monthly total income from TANF/wages - post-placement window	0.0013***	0.0002	<0.0001	1.001	0.0012***	0.0002	<0.0001	1.001	0.0013***	0.0002	<0.0001	1.001
Mother's percent average monthly total income from wages - post-placement window	-0.0109***	0.0025	<0.0001	0.989	-0.0111***	0.0031	0.0003	0.989	-0.0112***	0.0030	0.0002	0.989

Note: Comparison categories are listed first for each categorical variable. *** Significant at .001 level, ** at .01 level, * at .05 level, two-tailed test.

In summary, these comparisons show substantial differences between the WLW model and the Naïve model 1 and between the WLW model and the Naïve model 2 with respect to tests of statistical significance. The WLW model also differs from the Naïve model 2 with respect to the magnitude of the hazard ratios. Moreover, the factors that affect timing of reunification to a statistically significant degree in the WLW model differ from those identified by the two naïve models. These comparisons reveal that applying uncorrected models to grouped survival data produces misleading results, and underscore the importance of controlling for autocorrelation explicitly in a multilevel analysis of time-to-event data.

In this chapter, I briefly review the statistical literature on developing multilevel approaches to analyzing time-to-event data and show the application of one of such model (i.e., the WLW model) to correcting for autocorrelations introduced by sibling groups. I caution, however, that use of the WLW model may not always be an improvement over an uncorrected model. When a model is misspecified, that is, a model in which important explanatory variables are not included, and the analysis deletes too many subjects, differences between a WLW model and an uncorrected Cox model disappear. Misspecification causes changes in the estimated parameters and standard errors as a function of unobserved heterogeneity (Allison, 1995).

Indeed, use of the WLW model may be inappropriate if too many subjects are excluded from the analysis because the sample that is included in the analysis no longer represents the entire sample of interest. It is uncertain, however, how large a reduction renders use of the WLW model invalid. If loss of subjects is a concern, investigators may use the LWA procedure to correct for autocorrelation when they can justify its use.

7

Computing Software Packages for Survival Analysis

Alll commercial software packages offer procedures for survival analysis. Issues related to running some procedures have been discussed in relevant places in the book. In this chapter I provide an overview to highlight key issues in programming with *SAS*, *SPSS*, and *Stata*. Syntax files using *SAS*, and *Stata* packages to generate the examples in this book are available on the book's companion Web page. Readers may find them useful.

SAS

All survival procedures offered by *SAS* require the user to specify the value indicating censoring, not event. This feature is categorically different from *SPSS* and *Stata*. As a consequence, the user needs to be cautious in syntax specification when running the same data with different packages.

Proc Lifetest is the procedure to generate a life table including estimated hazard and survivor functions, the Kaplan-Meier estimation of survivor function, bivariate tests (i.e., log-rank, Wilcoxon's tests) on differences of survivor curves between groups, and graphics including the hazard plot, survivor plot, log-survivor plot, and log-log survivor plot (also known as log-cumulative-hazard plot). Additional graphic procedures such as **Proc gplot**, the macro **SMOOTH** written by Allison (1995), may be used to make the estimated curves smoother and more suitable for presentation.

Proc Logistic estimates a binary logistic regression, and **Proc Catmod** estimates a multinomial logit model. Hence, they are the procedures for discrete-time models. Before running *Proc Logistic* or *Proc Catmod*, the user needs to use programming commands to convert the person data into person-time data. For examples of data conversion, see Allison (1995) or syntax files available in the companion Web page for this book.

Proc Phreg is the procedure to estimate the Cox proportional hazards model. To run the model with time-varying covariates, the user needs to specify which variables indicate the time-varying information following the *Proc Phreg* statement and uses a series of "if...then" commands. The *BASELINE* key word in *Proc Phreg* may be used to generate the model-predicted survivor curves. *COVS(AGGREGATE)* is the key word to request the LWA or WLW marginal models; but for the WLW model, additional programming using *Proc IML* is required. The WLW macro created by Allison (1995) can also be used to run the model.

Proc lifereg is the procedure to estimate the parametric models. The *DISTRIBUTION* key word allows the user to specify different types of parametric models; the choices are *EXPONENTIAL* for the exponential model, *GAMMA* for the generalized or standard gamma model, *LOGISTIC* for the logistic model, *LLOGISTIC* for the log-logistic model, *LNORMAL* for the log-normal model, and *WEIBULL* for the Weibull model. To run the piecewise exponential model, the user specifies *DISTRIBUTION=EXPONENTIAL*, but it is necessary to run the procedure using the person-time data.

SPSS

SURVIVAL is the procedure to generate the life table and the hazard plot, survivor plot, log-survivor plot, and density (PDF) plot. *KM* estimates the Kaplan-Meier estimation of survivor function and generates similar plots. Both procedures offer bivariate tests (i.e., log-rank, Wilcoxon's tests).

LOGISTIC REGRESSION estimates the binary logistic regression (i.e., for the discrete-time model analyzing single event), and *NOMREG* estimates the multinomial logit model (i.e., for the discrete-time model analyzing multiple events).

COXREG is the procedure to run the Cox proportional hazards model. To specify time-varying covariates in the Cox regression, the user needs to use *TIME PROGRAM* before running *COXREG* to inform the program which variables contain time-varying information and how to create the time-varying covariates for the Cox model; typically this is done through a series of "if..." commands. To obtain model-predicted survivor curves, the user specifies *PLOT SURVIVAL*. This procedure only produces the curve using sample mean values of all independent variables, or curves defined by a categorical independent variable. Currently there is no procedure available to run multilevel analysis.

There is no procedure available to run the parametric models.

STATA

To run any procedure of survival analysis in *Stata*, the user needs to run *stset* first to inform the program of key variables and their roles in the analysis. Variables measuring the study time and the event code are defined at this stage. If the data file is saved, next time the user does not need to run *stset* again. *Stata* distinguishes between the single-record data (also known as a wide or multivariate file) and multiple-record data (also known as a long or univariate file), and this is a key feature *Stata* uses to run models with time-varying covariates. To run time-varying models, the user needs to organize the file in a multiple-record format. Using *stset*, the user informs the program of the ID variable so the program recognizes that within a same value of ID, records are for the same individual but at different times.

Several procedures can be used to conduct univariate, bivariate, and graphic analysis. *sts* is the procedure to generate, graph, list, and test the survivor functions (via the Kaplan-Meier estimator) and the Nelson-Aalen cumulative hazard function. *stci* computes means and percentiles of study time, and their standard errors and confidence intervals. *ltable* displays and graphs life tables for individual-level or aggregate data and provides the likelihood-ratio and log-rank tests to discern group differences.

The user needs to convert the person data into person-time data by using *Stata* programming commands before running a discrete-time model. Useful commands to fulfill this task include **expand, stsplit**, and a user-developed program called **prsnperd**. After creating the person-time data, **logistic** (for the binary logistic regression) or **mlogit** (for the multinomial logit model) may be employed to conduct the discrete-time analysis.

stcox is the procedure to conduct the Cox regression. As mentioned earlier, time-varying information and the structure of a multiple-record data file must be specified in **stset** before running **stcox**. Once this is done, the time-varying variables can be specified as other independent variables in the Cox regression without additional efforts. **stcoxkm** plots Kaplan-Meier observed survivor curves and compares them with Cox predicted curves. Thus, this is a procedure users can employ to check the proportionality assumption. In the *stcoxkm* curves, the closer the observed values are to the predicted values, the less likely it is that the proportional-hazards assumption has been violated. **stcurve** plots the survivor, hazard, or cumulative hazard functions based on an estimated Cox regression (i.e., the user runs it after running *stcox*). Note that *stcurve* provides all three types of curves, not just survivor curves. **stpower cox** is the procedure to conduct power analysis for the Cox regression and compute the needed sample size, power, and effect size for a Cox model. A set of **stcox postestimation** commands are of special interest after one runs *stcox*. The *vce(robust)* option can be used to request the robust variance estimator for a Cox regression, that is, to run the LWA model for multilevel analysis.

streg fits parametric survival models. *distribution ( )* is the key word to specify the parametric model of interest, and the choices are *(exponential)* for the exponential model, *(gompertz)* for the Gompertz model, *(loglogistic)* or *(llogistic)* for the log-logistic model, *(weibull)* for the Weibull model, *(lognormal)* or *(lnormal)* for the log-normal model, and *(gamma)* for the generalized gamma model. Like the procedure for SAS, the user specifies *(exponential)* based on person-time data to run the piecewise exponential model. **stcurve** following **streg** plots the model-based survivor, hazard, or cumulative hazard curves. A set of **streg postestimation** commands are of special interest after one runs *streg*.

8

Concluding Remarks

I n this chapter, I conclude by making a few remarks on criticisms of studies using survival analysis, and on directions for future development.

COMMON PITFALLS IN SURVIVAL ANALYSIS: A CHECKLIST FOR CRITICAL REVIEW

In statistical analysis, goodness criteria are not completely clear. Researchers often argue that the method must fit the research question and that assumptions must always be met as a test of statistical conclusion validity. Often we have choices in the selection of statistical methods and our choices should fit the data situation. Toward a better understanding of when and how to use a suitable survival model, I list below 12 pitfalls that can trip up empirical users when they use survival analysis.

1. *Inappropriate use of statistical models.* Perhaps the most obvious pitfall of all involves a mismatch of the research questions, the type of study data, and the statistical method. In the current context, it is not uncommon for a study's research questions to concern timing of event occurrence and the data to contain censoring of event times, but the

analyst does not employ a survival model. Wrong models not suitable to censored data include ANOVA, multiple regression analysis, and logistic regression.

2. *Incomplete description of key issues of survival models.* This happens when a study using survival analysis provides no information about the study window, metric of time (year, month, day, etc.), and origin of time. The study does not define censoring cases (or what type of censoring: right-hand, left-hand, or random censoring, or whether random censoring is informative) and provides no descriptive statistics about event history data such as proportion of subjects who were censored (or had events) during the study window.

3. *Inappropriate use of descriptive statistics for censored data, such as mean, standard deviation, and median.* Whenever the event times contain censored cases, the analyst should use median survivor function or quantiles from a life table or Kaplan-Meier estimator to describe the study data, and conduct bivariate analysis based on Greenwood's formula as well.

4. *Inappropriate treatment for left-hand censoring.* It's not uncommon that a survival analysis employs Cox regression to analyze data with left-hand censoring, and the study ignores the consequences of applying such a model to left-hand censored data.

5. *Failure to provide evidence to support the suitability of applying a parametric model.* In this case, the analyst uses parametric models but does not offer evidence to support the use of such models, particularly with regard to the distributional function of the study time.

6. *Mismatch between research questions and analytic model with regard to time-varying covariates.* In this case, testing time-varying covariates is implied by research questions, but the analysis fails to incorporate such covariates into the model. Additionally, the study does not test interaction of a time variable and a time-fixed covariate (i.e., fails to run a nonproportional hazard model) if such time-by-covariate interaction is strongly suggested by the study's substantive interest.

7. *Failure to correct for autocorrelation.* This pitfall occurs when a study employs clustered or autocorrelated survival times (e.g., survival times of

individuals from same family, neighborhood, or organization) but does not take the nesting structure of the data into consideration. The LWA, WLW, or frailty models should be employed in this context.

8. *Insufficient interpretation about interactive effects.* Significant interactive effects are often important findings and contribute to the knowledge base. It's not uncommon that the analyst presents regression coefficients (or hazard ratios) of the interaction terms in a table but fails to interpret the findings explicitly, efficiently, and effectively. Because interaction effects always involve three or more coefficients, the meaning of interaction (equivalently, buffering, moderating, and joint impact) is not self-evident from the coefficients or hazard ratios themselves. It is important to use graphic approaches or model-based simulations to interpret the interactive effects in a detailed fashion.

9. *Mismatch between research questions and analytic methods with regard to hypotheses involving mediational and moderating effects.* In this case, a study question clearly hypothesizes a mediational effect, but the analyst uses a method aiming to test an interactive or moderating effect in the analysis; or vice versa.

10. *Inadequacy in conducting model comparisons.* This pitfall occurs when a set of models were analyzed but the author fails to compare them with a suitable method or appropriate goodness-of-fit index. A common mistake in this context is that the analyst performed the likelihood ratio tests between non-nested models.

11. *Failure to conduct statistical power analysis.* In this case, the sample size employed by a study is small, but the researcher fails to offer evidence that the study has adequate power. Whenever a study uses a sample size below 50, the analyst should be cautious about its statistical power, conduct formal power analysis, and present results of the power analysis in conjunction with other findings.

12. *A wrong model is used in power analysis.* This pitfall occurs when the analyst uses a power analysis designed for other types of statistical analysis (i.e., not the kind of power analysis for survival data). Recall that the power analysis for survival models defines effect size as a hazard ratio. All other types of power analysis are not suitable for assessing the statistical power of models involving hazard ratios.

DIRECTIONS FOR FUTURE DEVELOPMENT

Over the past 30 years, methods of survival analysis have undergone a significant change, and much progress has been made in analyzing time-to-event data with various types of censoring, in facilitating a dynamic investigation between event time and time-varying covariates in various ways, in adjusting for clustering or autocorrelation so that a multilevel analysis of survival data is possible, and much more. Given the rapid development of new approaches and debate about existing methods, it is difficult to predict what the future may hold. However, I think that the following three directions are evident and are likely to contribute substantially to the advancement of survival analysis.

The first direction is a continuous development and improvement of approaches to handling clustered event times. Hougaard (2000, pp. 494–495) lists specific problems in this area that need to be resolved. For instance, the publicly available software for the frailty models can only handle the shared gamma and log-normal models and cannot evaluate the uncertainty of dependence. The asymptotic theory for multivariate failure time models needs to be developed. The frailty models need to address issues such as additive versus dominant inheritance, competing risks, single loci versus multi-loci dependence, and additive versus multiplicative frailty. The marginal modeling approach needs to be combined with the copula approach.

The second direction is to solidify the statistical theories of survival analysis by connecting the existing models (e.g., the Kaplan-Meier estimator and the Cox proportional hazards model) to the study of counting process and martingale theory (Therneau & Grambsch, 2000). For instance, linking the counting process theory to the Kaplan-Meier estimator is promising and fruitful; studies using such a theory have found that the Kaplan-Meier survivor functions are asymptotically normally distributed (Hosmer & Lemeshow, 1999). Research is needed in applying the counting process theory to prove the Nelson-Aalen estimator about the cumulative hazard function. The current survival analysis relies heavily on the Kaplan-Meier approach. Developing new survival models based on the Nelson-Aalen estimator is deemed promising (Therneau & Grambsch, 2000).

The third direction is a more innovative and wider application of the advanced survival models to solving research problems outside the field of biomedicine. Toward that end, social work research has made tremendous progress but continuous advancement is needed. Applying a multilevel approach to studying event recurrence is very much needed as the dominant analysis in the field focuses on only the first occurrence of an event. Competing risks analysis is another effective method that can be employed to address many substantively important questions. Combining survival analysis with new developments aiming at controlling for selection bias can improve the internal validity of many evaluation studies (Guo & Fraser, 2010).

Glossary

Age, Period, and Cohort Effects Three essential components or dimensions of longitudinal inquiry that play a vital role in understanding the effect of time on a particular outcome for an individual. Among the three effects, *age* reflects physiological change during a life process; *period* denotes the date of the outcome, and if the outcome varies with period whether the variation is likely due to some underlying factor that affects the outcome and varies in the same way for the entire population under study; and *cohort* refers to generational effects caused by factors that only affect particular groups when their outcome level changes with time.

Binary Logistic Regression A generalized linear model developed to analyze the determinants of a binary outcome variable. In such a nonlinear model, the dependent variable is not a linear function of the vector of the independent variables; however, by using an appropriate link function such as a logit function, the analyst expresses the model as a generalized linear model. The model is typically estimated by a maximum likelihood approach. In survival analysis, researchers employ the binary logistic regression to estimate a discrete-time-single-exit model.

Bivariate Analysis   Statistical analysis employs an independent-sample *t* test, or chi-square test, or correlation analysis, or analysis of variance (ANOVA) to examine the association between an outcome variable and an explanatory variable. Bivariate survival analysis should take data censoring into consideration. The following significance tests are special forms of bivariate analysis for time-to-event data: the log-rank test, the Wilcoxon test, the Breslow test, and the Tarone-Ware test.

Censoring   A special type of data incompletion. In survival analysis, censoring occurs when exact event times are known for only a portion of the study subjects, and the remainder of the event times is known only to exceed (or to be less than) a certain value. *Right-hand censoring* refers to the situation in which the ending point of a "spell" or episode is unknown, or the event of interest has not yet occurred at the end of data collection. *Left-hand censoring* refers to the situation in which the origin or the starting point of a spell is unknown. *Random censoring* refers to the situation in which the researcher observes both the origin and ending points, but the observation is terminated for reasons other than the event of interest.

Cox Proportional Hazards Model   Also known as the Cox regression. Using a *partial likelihood* method, it estimates the regression coefficients of the proportional hazards model by fully relying on the *ranks* of the event times. Advantages of this approach include its permission of analyzing time-to-event data without knowing the parametric nature of a survival distribution (hence, it's known as a distribution-free model), and permission of incorporating time-varying covariates in survival analysis. Recent advances and innovative models based on the Cox regression include competing risks analysis, creation of time-varying covariates that allow a time-fixed covariate to interact with event time, and multilevel survival analysis that handles data problem induced by clustering or autocorrelation.

Cox Regression   See Cox proportional hazards model.

Discrete-Time Models   Models that apply a binary logistic regression or a multinomial logit model to a well-defined person-time data set that pools together individuals' event histories, and use probability of event occurrence based on such data as a proxy of hazard rate to discern important predictors of the probability of event occurrence.

Distribution Function or Cumulative Distribution Function (CDF)   A popular statistic measuring a distribution. In survival analysis a CDF informs the probability that length of time T is less than or equal to any given value t. It is a definite integral of PDF, from time 0 (i.e., the onset of risk) to time t.

Duration Analysis or Transition Analysis   A different name of survival analysis typically used by economists.

Event History Analysis   A different name of survival analysis typically used by sociologists.

Failure-Time Analysis   A different name of survival analysis typically used by engineering researchers.

Frailty Models   See Multilevel Survival Analysis.

Graphic Approaches   Use plots of survival functions against time to discern the shape of study subjects' survival distribution, hazard rate, and differences on these functions between groups, and to check tenability of assumptions embedded in multivariate models so that the researcher can gauge whether applying a specific model is appropriate.

Hazard Function   Also known as *hazard rate*. A hazard function is an instantaneous probability measuring rate of change. It can be expressed as a ratio of conditional probability for the event to occur within an extremely small time interval (i.e., when the time interval approaches zero or is infinitesimal) over the time interval.

Informative Random Censoring   See Noninformative Random Censoring.

Integrated Hazard Function or Cumulative Hazard Function   The total number of subjects who would be expected to have the event up until time t. Formally, it is a definitive integral of the hazard function $h(t)$, from time 0 (i.e., the onset of risk) to time t.

Kaplan-Meier Estimator   Also known as the *product-limit* estimator. An analytic method to describe time-to-event data or to facilitate bivariate analysis of such data. It incorporates information from all the observations available, both uncensored and censored, by considering survival to any point in time as a series of steps defined by the observed survival and censored times. Greenwood's formula estimating the variance (hence the standard error) of survivor function allows analysts to compare survival distributions between groups to conduct a significance test.

Left-Hand Censoring   See Censoring.

Likelihood Ratio Test   A statistical test that evaluates which model fits the data better between two nested models. In conducting parametric survival analysis, researchers use this test to assess the suitability of a parametric model and to choose the most suitable one from several parametric models.

Life Table or Life-Table Method   An analytic method to describe time-to-event data. A life table is an extension of the traditional frequency table that displays hazard rates and survival functions from an empirical sample or population.

Longitudinal Inquiry   A research perspective or approach distinguishes itself from cross-sectional inquiry. The distinguishing feature of a longitudinal inquiry is that the response variable of interest and a set of explanatory variables in such studies are measured repeatedly over time. The main objective of a longitudinal inquiry is to characterize change in the response variable over time and to determine the covariates most associated with any change. Survival analysis is one of several statistical approaches facilitates longitudinal inquiry.

Marginal Models   See Multilevel Survival Analysis.

Methods to Handle Tied Event Times   Tied event times refer to the data situation in which two or more subjects have exactly the same value on study time. Methods developed to handle the tied times include the Breslow, exact, Efron, and discrete methods. The basic idea for all these methods is to consider true time-ordering among tied subjects.

Multilevel Survival Analysis   Also known as survival analysis of multivariate failure time data. A special type of survival analysis developed to correct for bias induced by clustering or nesting of survival times. Models to correct for autocorrelations of survival times fall into two broad categories: the frailty models and the marginal models. The frailty models require the user to specify correctly a parametric distribution of the frailty, and are best suited to clinical trials involving random selection of subjects or to samples involving matched-pairs covariates. The marginal models have much in common with the generalized estimating equation (GEE) approach that directly correct for estimated standard errors. The WLW and the LWA models are two marginal approaches proving to be popular among researchers of multilevel survival analysis.

Multinomial Logit Model   A generalized linear model developed to analyze the determinants of a nominal outcome variable. In such a nonlinear model, the dependent variable is not a linear function of the vector of the independent variables; however, by using an appropriate link function, the analyst expresses the model as a generalized linear model. The model is typically estimated by a maximum likelihood approach. In survival analysis, researchers employ the multinomial logit model to estimate a discrete-time-multiple-exits model. Such analysis of multiple exits is also known as analysis of competing risks.

Multivariate Analysis   Statistical analysis tests research hypotheses regarding the net impact of an explanatory variable on the outcome variable by controlling for all other explanatory variables. The ordinary least squares (OLS) regression is the most popular method of the multivariate analysis. Multivariate survival analysis should take data censoring into consideration, which includes discrete-time, Cox proportional hazards, and parametric models.

Noninformative Random Censoring   Survival models assume that random censoring is noninformative; that is, the censoring mechanism is under the researcher's control and is out of the study subject's control. When this assumption is violated, the researcher faces a data problem of *informative censoring*, under which condition study subjects would appear to have patterns among their event times, and there exists a systematic difference between the probability of having the defined event and the probability of being censored.

Nonparametric Method   A special type of survival analysis that does not have specific parameters (i.e., mathematically derived unknown quantities in the population) to describe the survival distribution. Examples of nonparametric methods are the life-table method, the Kaplan-Meier estimator, and the discrete-time model.

Ordinary Least Squares (OLS) Regression   The most important statistical method developed to answer research questions that are multivariate in nature. It aims to characterize the relationship between a continuous dependent variable and a set of independent or explanatory variables by using a least-squares estimation algorithm. The OLS regression serves as the foundation for advanced models and is the key to understanding multivariate survival analysis such as the discrete-time model, Cox regression, and the parametric models.

Parametric Method   A special type of survival analysis that explicitly uses parameters to describe the survival distribution (i.e., the distribution is known to have additional *shape* and *scale parameters* other than hazard rate, probability density function, cumulative distribution function, survival function, or cumulative hazard function). Examples of the parametric method are the exponential, Weibull, Gompertz, standard gamma, generalized gamma, log-normal, and log-logistic models. These multivariate models are developed by using a similar framework as OLS regression, but assume a parametric survival distribution for the study time and error term of the regression equation.

Partial Likelihood Estimator   An estimation algorithm developed to estimate the Cox regression. The estimator has the following important features: (a) the baseline hazard function in the model is canceled out; (b) as a result, the likelihood function is solely expressed by the coefficients to be estimated and the predictors; and (c) the model carefully takes the information of censored cases into account when building the likelihood function—censored cases are not excluded, and their information (i.e., the hazard functions) is built into the construction of the risk set.

Person-Level Data   See Person-Time Data.

Person-Time Data   A special type of data required by the discrete-time models. Unlike the most common type of person-level *data* in which each study subject contributes one and only one data line, the person-time data creates multiple data lines for each study subject based on the definitions of the study window, the time interval, censoring, and time-varying covariates.

Piecewise Exponential Model   A special type of parametric model that assumes piecewise constant hazard rates. It combines the exponential parametric model and the discrete-time model into one, and proves to be promising for many empirical data commonly found in social, health, and behavioral research.

Proportional Hazards Assumption   An assumption embedded in the Cox proportional hazards model. It states that the hazard for any individual in a sample is a fixed proportion of the hazard for any other individual, and the ratio of the two hazards is constant over time.

Probability Density Function (PDF)   A popular statistic measuring a distribution, commonly known as a frequency distribution. In survival analysis a PDF is similar to a hazard rate but the numerator of the formula is an unconditional probability.

Random Censoring   See Censoring.

Right-Hand Censoring   See Censoring.

Semiparametric Method   Also known as *distribution-free* method. A special type of survival analysis that makes assumptions about the hazard rate but does not use additional parameters to describe the distribution of survival times. The best example of the semiparametric method is the Cox proportional hazards model.

Survival Analysis   A collection of statistical methods aim to analyze timing of event occurrence and address questions that have to do with whether and when an event of interest takes place.

Survivor Function   An important function of survival analysis that measures the probability of not having the event (surviving to, or remaining in the subject set of having no event) by a particular time.

Time-to-Event Data   Data contain information about a well-defined time origin of a particular event and the time point at which such event occurs.

Time-Fixed Covariates   See Time-Varying Covariates.

Time-Varying Covariates   Also known as time-dependent covariates. These are the independent variables that change values over the course of observation. In contrast, independent variables that do not change value over time are called time-fixed, or time-constant, or time-independent covariates. Incorporating time-varying covariates in a survival analysis makes the investigation truly dynamic, that is, it looks into the relationship between the timing of the event occurrence and an independent variable from a truly changing perspective.

Univariate Analysis   Statistical analysis employs mean, median, and standard deviation to discern central tendency and dispersion of the study variables. Univariate survival analysis should take data censoring into consideration, which includes estimation of hazard and survivor functions from the life-table method and estimation of survivor function from the Kaplan-Meier estimator.

Notes

CHAPTER 2

1. Note that this function is called "survivor function," not "survival function." The difference signifies that the function specifically measures the probability of survivors, that is, the probability of not having had the event (i.e., "survived" to) at a given time point t.
2. Different software packages define the plot slightly differently. *SAS Proc Lifetest* defines the vertical axis as $\log[-\log \hat{S}(t)]$, while *Stata stphplot* defines it as $-\log[-\log \hat{S}(t)]$, though both packages use $\log t$ as the horizontal axis.

CHAPTER 4

1. In the prior section, the illustrating model does not contain an interaction term whereas the current model does.

CHAPTER 6

1. The issue of intragroup correlation is more complicated in survival analysis than in other longitudinal studies because of censoring. The method of assigning maximum length of stay to subjects whose lengths of study are longer than the study window, as we recommend here, is an informal procedure.
2. Liang et al. (1993) developed another marginal model, the "LSC" model, which is basically the same as the LWA model (Lin, 1994). It employs the same estimating function as that of the LWA, but replaces the ratio of survival functions in estimating the "score function" by an analog that exploits pairwise comparisons of independent observations.

3. Wei et al. (1989) employ a sample of 36 patients with approximately three distinct event times for each patient.

4. Lin's Monte Carlo simulation shows that the LWA-type model tends to be more efficient than the WLW-type model when failure times are generated with a common baseline hazard function, but the difference is very small. His study using real clinical data shows that the LSC model produces parameter estimates very similar to those of the WLW model, and the standard error estimates are almost identical between the two (Lin, 1994).

References

Allison, P. D. (1982). Discrete-time methods for the analysis of event histories. In S. Leighhardt (Ed.), *Sociological Methodology 1982* (pp. 61–98). San Francisco, CA: Jossey-Bass.

Allison, P. D. (1995). *Survival analysis using the SAS system*. Cary, NC: SAS Institute.

Andersen, P. K., & Gill, R. D. (1982). Cox's regression model for counting processes: A large sample study. *Annals of Statistics, 10*, 1100–1120.

Bane, M. J., & Ellwood, D. T. (1994). Welfare realities: From rhetoric to reform. Cambridge, MA: Harvard University Press.

Baron, R., & Kenny, D. (1986). The moderator-mediator variable distinction in social psychological research: Conceptual, strategic, and statistical considerations. *Journal of Personality and Social Psychology, 51*(6), 1173–1182.

Benedict, M. I., & White, R. B. (1991). Factors associated with foster care length of stay. *Child Welfare, 70*, 45–58.

Benedict, M. I., White, R. B., & Stallings, R. (1987). Race and length of stay in foster care. *Social Work Research and Abstracts, 23*, 23–26.

Brown, E. L. (2005). *The role of individual and community characteristics in child welfare placement decisions.* Unpublished doctoral dissertation, University of North Carolina, Chapel Hill.

Brown, S. L. (2000). Union transitions among cohabitors: The significance of relationship assessments and expectations. *Journal of Marriage and the Family, 62*, 833–846.

Clayton, D., & Cuzick, J. (1985). Multivariate generalizations of the proportional hazards model. *Journal of the Royal Statistical Society, Series A, 148, Part 2,* 82–117.

Cleves, M. A., Gould, W. W., & Gutierrez, R. G. (2004). *An introduction to survival analysis using Stata* (Rev. ed.). College Station, TX: Stata Press.

Cohen, J. (1988). *Statistical power analysis for the behavioral sciences* (2nd ed.). Hillsdale, NJ: Lawrence Erlbaum Associates.

Collett, D. (1994). *Modelling survival data in medical research*. London: Chapman & Hall.

Courtney, M. E. (1994). Factors associated with the reunification of foster children with their families. *Social Service Review, 68,* 81–108.

Courtney, M. E. (1995). Reentry to foster care of children returned to their families. *Social Service Review, 69,* 226–241.

Courtney, M. E., & Wong, Y. I. (1996). Comparing the timing of exits from substitute care. *Children and Youth Services Review, 18*(4/5), 307–334.

Cox, D. R. (1972). Regression models and life tables (with discussion). *Journal of the Royal Statistical Society, B, 74,* 187–220.

Dattalo, P. (2008). *Determining sample size: Balancing power, precision, and practicality.* New York: Oxford University Press.

Dupont, W. D., & Plummer, W. D., Jr. (2004). *PS: Power and sample size calculation,* Retrieved on January 1, 2009, from http://biostat.mc.vanderbilt.edu/twiki/bin/view/Main/PowerSampleSize

Evans, M., Hastings, N., & Peacock, B. (2000). *Statistical distributions* (3rd ed.). New York: John Wiley.

Everitt, B. S. (2005a). History of medical statistics. In B. S. Everitt & C. R. Palmer (Eds.), *The encyclopaedic companion to medical statistics.* London: Hodder Education.

Everitt, B. S. (2005b). Longitudinal data. In B. S. Everitt & C. R. Palmer (Eds.), *The encyclopaedic companion to medical statistics.* London: Hodder Education.

Fienberg, S. E., & Mason, W. M. (1979). Identification and estimation of age-period-chohort models in the analysis of discrete archival data. *Sociological Methodology, 1978,* 1–67.

Fisher, R. A. (1935/1971). *The design of experiments.* Edinburgh, UK: Oliver & Boyd.

Fraser, M. W., Jenson, J. M., Kiefer, D., & Popuang, C. (1994). Statistical methods for the analysis of critical life events. *Social Work Research, 18*(3), 163–177.

Fraser, M. W., Pecora, P. J., Popuang, C., & Haapala, D. A. (1992). Event history analysis: A proportional hazards perspective on modeling outcomes in intensive family preservation services. *Journal of Social Service Research, 16,* 123–158. Fraser, M. W., Walton, E., Lewis, R. E., Pecora, P. J., & Walton, W. K. (1996). An experiment in family reunification: Correlates of outcomes at one-year follow-up. *Children and Youth Services Review, 18*(4/5), 335–361.

Glisson, C., Bailey, J. W., & Post, J. A. (2000). Predicting the time children spend in state custody. *Social Service Review, 74,* 253–280.

Goerge, R. M. (1990). The reunification process in substitute care. *Social Service Review, 64*(3), 422–457.

Greene, W. H. (2003). *Econometric analysis* (5th ed.). Upper Saddle River, NJ: Prentice Hall.

Guo, S. (1992). *Data management in event history analysis—using SPSS.* Paper presented at the 1992 SPSS Academic Conference, Seattle, WA.

Guo, S. (2008). Quantitative research. In T. Mizrahi and L. E. Davis (Eds.), *Encyclopedia of social work* (20th ed.). New York: Oxford University Press.

Guo, S., Barth, R. P., & Gibbons, C. (2006). Propensity score matching strategies for evaluating substance abuse services for child welfare clients. *Children and Youth Services Review, 28,* 357–383.

Guo, S., Biegel, D., Johnson, J., & Dyches, H. (2001) Assessing the impact of mobile crisis services on preventing hospitalization: A community-based evaluation. *Psychiatric Services, 52,* 223–228.

Guo, S., & Fraser, W. M. (2010). *Propensity score analysis: Statistical methods and applications.* Thousand Oaks, CA: Sage.

Guo, G., & Rodriguez, G. (1992). Estimating a multivariate proportional hazards model for clustered data using the EM algorithm, with an application to child survival in Guatemala. *Journal of the American Statistical Association, 87,* 969–976.

Guo, S., & Wells, K. (2003). Research on timing of foster-care outcomes: One methodological problem and approaches to its solution. *Social Service Review, 77*(1), 1–24.

Harris, K. M. (1993). Work and welfare among single mothers in poverty. *American Journal of Sociology, 99*(2), 317–352.

Heckman, J. J., & Singer, B. (1985). *Longitudinal analysis of labor market data.* Cambridge, UK: Cambridge University Press.

Hegar, R. L. (1988). Sibling relationships and separations: Implications for child placement. *Social Service Review, 62*(3), 446–467.

Holford, T. R. (2005). Age-period cohort analysis. In B. S. Everitt & C. R. Palmer (Eds.), *The encyclopaedic companion to medical statistics.* London: Hodder Education.

Hosmer, D. W., & Lemeshow, S. (1989). *Applied logistic regression.* New York: John Wiley.

Hosmer, D. W., & Lemeshow, S. (1999). *Applied survival analysis: Regression modeling of time to event data.* New York: John Wiley.

Hougaard, P. (1986). Survival models for heterogeneous populations derived from stable distributions. *Biometrika, 73,* 387–396.

Hougaard, P. (1987). Modeling multivariate survival. *Scandinavian Journal of Statistics, 14,* 291–304.

Hougaard, P. (2000). *Analysis of multivariate survival data.* New York: Springer-Verlag.

Hsieh, F. Y., & Lavori, P. W. (2000). Sample size calculations for the Cox proportional hazards regression models with nonbinary covariates. *Controlled Clinical Trials, 21,* 552–560.

Kemp, S. P., & Bodonyi, J. M. (2000). Infants who stay in foster care: Child characteristics and permanency outcomes of legally free children first placed as infants. *Child and Family Social Work, 5*(2), 95–106.

Klein, J. P. (1992). Semiparametric estimation of random effects using the Cox model based on the EM algorithm. *Biometrics, 48,* 795–806.

Kutner, M. H., Nachtsheim, C. J., & Neter, J. (2004). *Applied linear regression models* (4th ed.). New York: McGraw Hill/Irwin.

Lawless, J. F. (1982). *Statistical models and methods for lifetime data.* New York: John Wiley.

Lee, E. W., Wei, L. J., & Amato, D. A. (1992). Cox-type regression analysis for large numbers of small groups of correlated failure time observations. In J. P. Klein & P. K. Goel (Eds.), *Survival analysis: State of the art* (pp. 237–247). Dordrecht: Kluwer Academic.

Liang, K.Y., Self, S. G., & Chang, Y. C. (1993). Modeling marginal hazards in multivariate failure time data. *Journal of the Royal Statistical Society, Series B, 55,* 441–453.

Lichter, D. T., Qian, Z., & Mellott, L. M. (2006). Marriage or dissolution? Union transitions among poor cohabiting women. *Demography, 43,* 223–240.

Lin, D. Y. (1994). Cox regression analysis of multivariate failure time data: The marginal approach. *Statistics in Medicine, 13,* 2233–2247.

Long, J. S. (1997). Regression models for categorical and limited dependent variables. Thousand Oaks, CA: Sage.

Lopoo, L. M., & Western, B. (2005). Incarceration and the formation and stability of marital unions. *Journal of Marriage and Family, 67,* 721–734.

McCullaph, P., & Nelder, J. (1989). *Generalized linear models* (2nd ed.). London: Chapman & Hall.

McMurtry, S. L., & Lie, G. Y. (1992). Differential exit rates of minority children in foster care. *Social Work Research and Abstracts, 28*(1), 42–48.

Nielsen, G. G., Gill, R. D., Andersen, P. K., & Sorensen, T. I. A. (1992). A counting process approach to maximum likelihood estimation in frailty models. *Scandinavian Journal of Statistics, 19,* 25–43.

Oakes, D. (1989). Bivariate survival models induced by frailties. *Journal of the American Statistical Association, 84,* 487–493.

Oakes, D. (1992). Frailty models for multiple event times. In J. P. Klein & P. K. Goel (Eds.), *Survival analysis: State of the Art.* Netherlands: Kluwer.

Osborne, C., Manning, W. D., & Smock, P. J. (2004). *Instability in fragile families: The role of race-ethnicity, economics, and relationship quality.* Unpublished working paper 2004-17-FF. Princeton, NJ: Center for Research on Child Well-Being.

Prentice, R. L., Williams, B. J., & Peterson, A. V. (1981). On the regression analysis of multivariate failure time data. *Biometrika, 68,* 373–379.

Raudenbush, S. W., & Bryk, A. S. (2002). *Hierarchical linear models: Applications and data analysis methods* (2nd ed.). Thousands Oaks, CA: Sage.

RTI. (2002). *SUDAAN: User manual release 8.0.* Research Triangle Park, NC: Research Triangle Institute.

Sandefur, G. D., & Cook, S. T. (1998). Permanent exits from public assistance: The impact of duration, family, and work. *Social Forces, 77*(2), 763–786.

Schoenfeld, D. (1983). Sample-size formula for the proportional-hazards regression model. *Biometrics, 39,* 499–503.

Shook, K. (1999). Does the loss of welfare income increase the risk of involvement with the child welfare system? *Children and Youth Services Review, 21*(9–10), 781–814.

Singer, J. D., & Willett, J. B. (2003). *Applied longitudinal data analysis: Modeling change and event occurrence.* New York: Oxford University Press.

Smith, M. C. (1996). An exploratory survey of foster mother and caseworker attitudes about sibling placement. *Child Welfare, 75*(4), 357–375.

Staff, I., & Fein, E. (1992). Together or separate: A study of siblings in foster care. *Child Welfare, 71*(3), 257–270.

StataCorp. (2007). *ST: Survival analysis and epidemiological tables, release 10.* College Station, TX: StataCorp.

Therneau, T. M., & Grambsch, P. M. (2000). *Modeling survival data: Extending the Cox model.* New York: Springer-Verlag.

Tuma, N. B., & Hannan, M. T. (1984). *Social dynamics: Models and methods.* Orlando, FL: Academic Press.

UCLA Academic Technology Services. (2008). FAQ: What are pseudo R-squareds? Retrieved April 28, 2008. from http://www.ats.ucla.edu/stat/mult_pkg/faq/general/Psuedo_RSquareds.htm

Wei, L. J., Lin, D. Y., & Weissfeld, L. (1989). Regression analysis of multivariate incomplete failure time data by modeling marginal distributions. *Journal of the American Statistical Association, 84*(408), 1065–1073.

Wells, K., & Guo, S. (1999). Reunification and reentry of foster children. *Children and Youth Services Review, 21*(4), 273–294.

Wells, K., & Guo, S. (2003). Mothers' welfare and work income and reunification with children in foster care. *Children and Youth Services Review, 25*(3), 203–224.

Wells, K., & Guo, S. (2004). Reunification of foster children before and after welfare reform. *Social Service Review, 78*(1), 74–95.

Wells, K., & Guo, S. (2006). Welfare reform and child welfare outcomes: A multiple-cohort study. *Children and Youth Services Review,* 28, 941–960.

Wikipedia. (2008). Heraclitus. Retrieved on December 20, 2008, from http://en.wikipedia.org/wiki/Heraclitus#cite_note-22

Yamaguchi, K. (1991). *Event history analysis.* Newbury Park, CA: Sage.

Zeger, S. L., Liang, K.Y., & Albert, P. S. (1988). Models for longitudinal data: A generalized estimating equation approach. *Biometrics, 44,* 1049–1060.

Index

Adoption, 28, 69

AFDC. *See* Aid to Families with Dependent Children

Age effects, in longitudinal inquiry, 9, 138

Aid to Families with Dependent Children (AFDC), 23–24, 107

Allison, P., 29, 33, 57, 76, 78, 80, 82, 89, 94, 95, 99, 104, 118, 124, 125, 130

Analysis of Variance (ANOVA), 4, 119, 124, 134

ANOVA. *See* Analysis of Variance

Autocorrelation, 9, 22, 116, 119, 134–35, 139, 141
  coefficient for event time assessment, 119–20
  consequences of using, 117–18
  intragroup correlation assessment, 119
  problem diagnosis, 123–24
  problem scope assessment, 118–19

Bailey, J. W., 20–21t

Baseline hazard function, 76, 121, 143

Benedict, M. I., 11t

BHHH. *See* B-triple-H model

Binary logistic regression, 56, 58, 63–66, 68t, 72, 75–76, 80, 130, 131, 138, 139

Biomedical research, 5, 116, 117

Bivariate analysis, 4, 37, 42, 48, 51, 55, 129, 139, 140

Bodonyi, J. M., 21t

Breslow test, 47, 51, 80, 139, 141

B-triple-H (BHHH) model, 64

Buffering effects. *See* Interactive effects

CDF. *See* Cumulative Distribution Function

Censoring, 3–4, 26–29, 40, 51, 58, 61, 77, 108, 134, 136, 140, 143, 144, 145n1
  informative random, 28–29, 118, 134
  interval, 29, 98, 99
  left-hand, 27, 28, 30, 98, 99, 134
  length of time, 31t
  noninformative random, 28, 29, 142
  problem, longitudinal inquiry addressing of, 9
  random, 27–29, 30, 69, 70, 118, 134, 139
  right-hand, 27, 28, 30, 70, 94, 134